HOW THE MASS CAME TO BE

From the Last Supper to Today's Eucharist

Pierre Loret, C.SS.R.

Translated by Dorothy Marie Zimmerman, SSND, and adapted by Mary Terese Donze, ASC

One Liguori Drive
Liguori, Missouri 63057
(314) 464-2500

Imprimi Potest:
John F. Dowd, C.SS.R.
Provincial, St. Louis Province
Redemptorist Fathers

Imprimatur:
+ Edward J. O'Donnell
Vicar General, Archdiocese of St. Louis

ISBN 0-89243-212-8

Contents

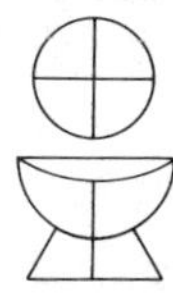

1

What We Do in His Memory

In the 1970s, young Americans enjoyed the ballads of singer-composer Neil Diamond. In "Morningside," a song on his *Moods* album, Neil Diamond tells about a little old man who died. The old man died and no one cried. He left behind "a table made of nails and pride." And on the table he carved these words: *"For My Children."*

Sadly, no one ever claimed that table. The man and his gift were forgotten.

This booklet is about another person who died and left a gift — a gift that *was* remembered. This Man died young. He, too, had a table — the one at which He sat when He shared His Last Supper. And there were nails — the ones that pierced His hands and feet as He died on a cross. This Man, too, left us a message about His gift. The message is: *"Do this in memory of me."*

The Man, Jesus, is still among us; He is risen from the dead. We meet Him face-to-face in love each time we gather to "Do this" in His memory. What we do in His memory is called Eucharist. This booklet tells the 2,000-year-old story of what Catholic Christians have done with that gift.

Sidon
Mt. Hermon
Tyre
Caesarea Philippi
Mediterranean Sea
GALILEE
Chorazin
Capernaum
Cana
Sea of Galilee
Nazareth
Mt. Tabor
Caesarea Maritima
SAMARIA
River Jordan
Gerasa
Sebaste
Antipatris
Joppa
Jericho
Jerusalem
Qumran
Bethlehem
Herodion
Machaerus
Dead Sea
JUDAEA
Masada
IDUMAEA
NABATAEA

What the Gospels Tell Us about Jesus

The Gospels tell us that Jesus was born at Bethlehem in Judea, a village in southern Palestine. They also say that He grew up in Nazareth, a small town up north in Galilee.

The Gospels do not tell us how Jesus spent His childhood. But they do tell us that when He was twelve, He went with His parents, Mary and Joseph, to Jerusalem to worship in the Temple. Like any true Jew, Jesus loved the Temple. And being the Son of God, He felt at home in this great place of worship — "His Father's house."

When Jesus was about thirty years old, He began preaching the Good News. Many people believed in Jesus. No one, they said, had ever spoken the way He did. No one had ever done the marvelous things He did. He gave sight to the blind, made deaf people hear again, cured lepers, even brought dead people back to life. Everyone talked about the great prophet from Galilee.

Jesus heard some of the things people were saying about Him, and one day He asked His twelve Apostles: "Who do people say that the Son of Man is?"

They answered, "Some say John the Baptizer, others Elijah, still others Jeremiah or one of the prophets."

Jesus listened. Then He turned to them and asked, "And you . . . who do you say that I am?"

Peter — his name means "rock" — answered at once. "You are the Messiah . . . the Son of the living God!"

Jesus did not deny it. Instead, He turned to Peter and said, "I for my part declare to you, you are 'Rock,' and on this rock I will build my church. . . . " (Matthew 16:13,14,15,18)

This is the first time in the Gospels that Jesus speaks of His Church, the community that lives and grows by remembering Him in the Eucharist.

Preparing for the Last Supper

Jesus had been traveling and preaching for about three years. At the end of that time He knew He was going to be put to death, knew that He would be rejected, condemned, and crucified. He also knew that this was going to happen during the Passover feast. Even now, two of His Apostles, Peter and John, were asking Him, "Where do you wish us to go to prepare the Passover supper for you?" (Mark 14:12)

Jesus said to them, "Go into the city and you will come upon a man carrying a water jar. Follow him. Whatever house he enters, say to the owner, 'The Teacher asks, Where is my guest room where I may eat the Passover with my disciples?' " (Mark 14:13-14)

These were strange directions. Men did not carry water pitchers; in those days that was a woman's job. But the two Apostles had scarcely reached the city when they saw a young man with a pitcher of water pushing his way through the crowds. They followed him to the room we call the Cenacle (*cena* is the Latin word for supper). Here they made their preparations. Here, in this room, Jesus ate His Last Supper with His Apostles.

The First Eucharist

Toward evening, Jesus and the Apostles met in the Cenacle. As He sat at table, Jesus said to His friends, "I have greatly desired to eat this Passover with you before I suffer." (Luke 22:15)

During the Supper, Jesus took bread and gave thanks. Then He broke the bread and gave it to the Apostles. Jesus' words over the bread and wine are recorded in four places in the Bible — Matthew (chapter 26), Mark (chapter 14), Luke (chapter 22), Paul's First Letter to the Corinthians (chapter 11). Each of the four versions is slightly different from the others. And down through the cen-

turies, in the Eastern and Western churches, there have been dozens of other slight variations. Remember, too, that Jesus spoke a language called Aramaic — not English. The wording we have today in the Eucharistic Prayer (II) is as follows:

Before he was given up to death,
a death he freely accepted,
he took bread and gave you thanks.
He broke the bread,
gave it to his disciples, and said:
Take this, all of you, and eat it:
this is my body which will be given up for you.

When supper was ended, he took the cup.
Again he gave you thanks and praise,
gave the cup to his disciples, and said:

Take this, all of you, and drink from it:
this is the cup of my blood,
the blood of the new and everlasting covenant.
It will be shed for you and for all
so that sins may be forgiven.
Do this in memory of me.

These are the words we use in liturgy to remember the Last Supper — the first Christian Eucharist.

PART ONE

The Mass in the Early Church

(From the Last Supper to A.D. 604)

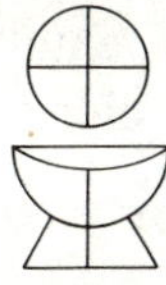

2

The Eucharist of the Apostles

After Jesus died, and even after He ascended into heaven, the Apostles were afraid. They feared that they, too, might be killed. But after the Holy Spirit came upon them at Pentecost, filling them with courage and understanding, they remembered: *"Do this in memory of me."*

Now they asked themselves, How shall we do this remembering? One of the questions that needed answering was: *Is the Eucharist part of the regular Jewish prayer in the Temple?*

At first it seemed that it was. After they finished their prayers in the Temple, the Apostles would return home and celebrate Eucharist. The Temple services seemed to be a natural, prayerful beginning for the Mass.

But one day as they were entering the Temple, Peter and John cured a lame man in the name of Jesus. The leaders of the Jews were furious; they had forbidden anyone ever to mention the name of Jesus in the Temple. Soon these leaders forbade the Apostles ever to enter the Temple again. These same men put Peter in prison, and they stoned to death a deacon named Stephen. Eventually, Jesus' followers stopped praying in the Temple, and decided: *Christian Eucharist is not part of Jewish prayer.*

Another question the Apostles had to deal with was: *How do people qualify to take part in the Mass?*

A great many of Jesus' early followers after Pentecost were Jews from Jerusalem. They were pious people who loved their Jewish prayers and customs. But many of Saint Paul's newly converted Christians were Gentiles — non-Jews. Soon some of the Christian Jews began to insist that any Gentile who wanted to become a follower of Christ should first become a Jew.

Saint Paul disagreed. He said that in order to be a Christian and to take part in Christian Eucharist just one thing was necessary: *Baptism*.

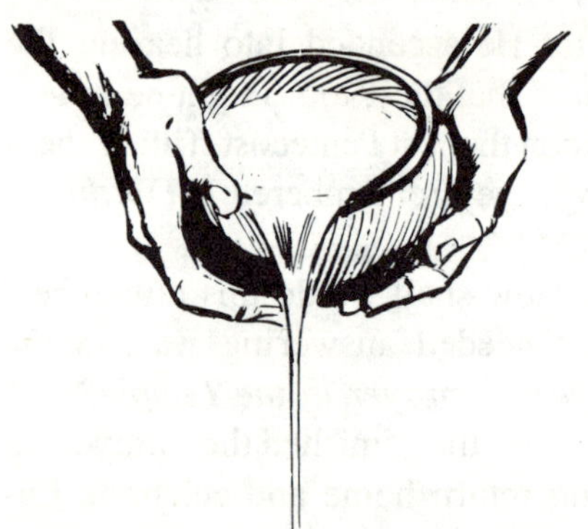

To settle the argument, Peter, Paul, James, and the other Apostles and elders held a meeting in Jerusalem. Finally, they decided: *Any baptized Christian — man, woman, pagan, slave, anyone — could take part in the Eucharist*. Paul had won the argument.

There were other problems to settle, such as: *When* should the Mass be celebrated? And *where?*

The early Church decided to have the Mass on Sunday because that was the day Jesus rose from the dead. And even before they stopped attending Jewish services, the early Christians shared Eucharist in each other's homes.

There were various other decisions that the early Church had to make. In each case the Holy Spirit guided the Apostles in carrying out Jesus' words, "Do this in memory of me."

3

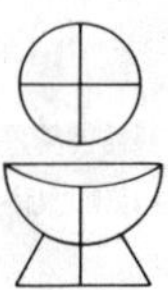

The Eucharist in Times of Persecution

The early Christians lived in a world ruled by pagan Rome. The Romans had their own gods. When the Christians refused to worship these gods, the Romans persecuted the Christians. These persecutions began about A.D. 64 and continued, off and on, until A.D. 313. Many men, women, and children were cruelly martyred for Christ.

Tradition

During this time of persecution, a great number of Christians went into hiding. This explains why not much information about the Eucharist comes to us from this period. However, we do know that the early Christians kept true to the teaching they had received from the Apostles. They passed on this teaching to their children, and those children told their children. (Teaching passed on in this way is called *tradition*.)

After a while some of the Christians feared that not enough of them would be left alive to pass on the tradition. To make sure that others coming after them would act as the Apostles did and as

Christ wanted them to do, these Christians began to write down what they were doing. One of these writings was discovered in the city of Constantinople (Istanbul) in 1875. The document was titled *The Teaching of the Twelve Apostles,* and seems to have been written about the year 100. In the early third century, Saint Hippolytus, a priest who lived in Rome, also wrote a book that he called *The Tradition of the Apostles.*

Unity in Diversity

One of the things we learn from these early writings is that the priest who led at the Eucharist could make up most of his own prayers. Since this was so, probably no two priests prayed the same prayers. In other words, there was *great diversity* — a great deal of difference — in the way the Eucharist was prayed. However, when it came to the consecration of the bread and wine, each priest repeated Christ's words just as our priests do today. On this one point there was *unity.*

Unity and diversity are not words that have to do only with the Eucharist. Think of the human body. The eye is different from the ear, and the ear differs from the toe. That is diversity. But all these parts form one body. That is unity. Or take the family. Each member differs from the other. That is diversity. But they all form one family. That is unity.

This unity and diversity both in the celebration of Eucharist and in other Christian practices was common in the early Church. In the third century a man named Firmilian, who was bishop of Caesarea in Palestine, made a journey from country to country. Along the way, Firmilian noticed many differences in Christian practice. Stopping in Rome, he wrote the following lines:

"Not only in the celebration of Easter, but in many other points, the Romans have their own customs, different from those of Jerusalem. In most of the countries, according to the *diversity* of places and people, many things are different. But in spite of this, nothing draws the people away from the peace and *unity* of the Catholic Church."

The Language of the Eucharist

By the middle of the third century many Christians were not able to understand Greek, the language in which the Eucharist was prayed. They spoke and understood Latin. Saint Callistus, who was bishop of Rome at the time, told his priests to begin celebrating the Eucharist in Latin so that people could follow what was going on.

At first not everyone wanted to make this change. In churches where many of the Christians were Greek, the priests were slow to adapt to the new regulation. In the end, the churches of Rome made the change. Except for a few Greek words, the Eucharist in Rome was prayed in Latin.

Authority of the Pope

When Saint Callistus, the bishop of Rome, told priests to begin celebrating the liturgy in Latin, the priests obeyed him. An earlier bishop of Rome, Saint Clement, had criticized the Christians of Corinth, a city in Greece, about the way they behaved during the Eucharist. In that case, too, the people obeyed the bishop of Rome and changed their ways. The people listened to these two bishops because they had special authority. Through the ages, the bishop of Rome has been recognized as the chief bishop, the pope. This is why, when Callistus and Clement made regulations for celebrating the liturgy, the Christians obeyed.

Living the Eucharist

The early Christians suffered much for their belief in Christ. That is one reason the Eucharist meant so much to them. It brought them Christ. The worst punishment they could suffer was to be judged unworthy of communion, for the Eucharist gave them joy and courage.

The Eucharist also created a bond of *unity* among believers. No matter how far away from one another the Christian communities were, they were *one* in the love and worship of Christ.

It was dangerous to celebrate the Eucharist during the times of persecution. Because of the danger, Christians who came to the Sunday Eucharist would be permitted to take home some of the consecrated bread — the Body of Christ. They could then receive the Lord in their homes during the week. They also carried communion to the sick. Some even risked sneaking communion into prisons to Christians who were to be executed as martyrs for their faith.

Even children did daring things for Christ. One boy named Tarcisius begged a priest to let him take communion to some Christians who were condemned to die. On his way to the prison, a group of pagan boys met Tarcisius and tried to snatch what he was carrying. The boys never got hold of the sacred Host because someone came along and broke up the fight. But it was too late for Tarcisius. The boys had beaten him to death. The heroism of this young martyr is an example of how the life of the early Christians was centered on the Eucharist.

4

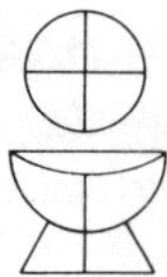

The Golden Age of Liturgy

Up until the year 313, Christians in many parts of the Roman Empire had to live in hiding much of the time. Suddenly, in the year 313, everything changed for them. Not only were they allowed to practice their faith freely but the emperor himself became a Christian. Everything was so wonderful for the Christians that historians have called this period the *Golden Age*. It began with the reign of Emperor Constantine in 313, and ended with the death of Pope Saint Gregory the Great in 604.

The Final Persecution

In the year 303, the Emperor Diocletian began the last and most brutal of the persecutions. His goal was complete extermination of all Christians. Priests and deacons, Christian soldiers and court officials, anyone who professed Christianity, were arrested, tortured, and executed. In the West the persecution stopped in 305. But in the East it raged on, reaching its peak between the years 305 and 311. The number of martyrs was very high.

In April of 311 the new ruler, Galerius, realized that the persecution was a failure; he brought it to a halt with his famous Edict of Toleration, which declared: " . . . may they from now on be Christians." Christianity was no longer against the law.

The Emperor Constantine

In 312, a young general named Constantine came south across the Alps and overcame the latest Roman emperor, Maxentius. The story is told that on the night before battle, Constantine saw a large cross in the sky. Circling the cross were these words: "In this sign you shall conquer." Since the cross was the symbol or sign of Christianity, Constantine gave credit for his victory to the prayers of his Christian mother and Christian soldiers.

The Emperor Constantine presents the tiara to Pope Sylvester I.

After his victory at the Milvian Bridge, Constantine became emperor. He declared himself a Christian and supported Christianity in every way. The next year, 313, he published a famous document which is called the *Edict of Milan*. Galerius had made Christianity legal. Constantine now gave it full equality with all the other religions. But Constantine did even more. He donated great buildings to be used as Christian churches. Some were so magnificent that they were called *basilicas* — royal buildings.

For about 250 years, it had been common for small groups of Christians to meet in underground cemeteries called *catacombs* or in secret hiding places. Now they had legally approved churches in which several thousands could gather at once. Instead of dark, damp underground caves, they had beautiful buildings filled with priceless works of art.

All this had its effect on Christian worship. The Eucharist became surrounded with pomp and splendor.

Growth of Church Influence

After Constantine became emperor, he left Italy and moved his court to Turkey, where he built a new city, Constantinople, in honor of himself. This new city became the political center of the East.

Rome, the city of the former emperors, was left in the hands of the pope. Christians and pagans alike turned to the pope. He was not only head of Christianity and guardian of the faith but also the guide and defender of the city. One of the popes laughingly said, "I no longer know whether I am pope or emperor." The other bishops, too, served as political leaders as well as spiritual guides.

It was about this time that the Church in Rome and the surrounding countries came to be known as the Western Church. In Constantinople and its neighboring territory, the Christians were known as the Eastern or Greek Church.

Outstanding Leaders

For several centuries after the Age of Persecution, God gave the Church some of its greatest saints. In the Eastern Church were Saints Athanasius, John Chrysostom, and Basil. In the West, there were Saints Ambrose, Augustine, Jerome, and later, Gregory the Great.

These outstanding Christian leaders saved the Church from a new paganism that hordes of barbarians were spreading over Europe. They also defended the Church against *heresy* — false teaching. They defended particularly against the heresy of Arius, a priest who denied that Christ is God. This false teaching struck at the very heart of Christian life, the Eucharist.

Saint Gregory the Great

Saint Gregory was elected pope in 590. By that time many developments had taken place in the Eucharist. Gregory tried to put these developments into organized form for his Roman churches. He was so successful that when he died in 604 the Roman *liturgy* — public worship — was already well established.

Some changes Gregory made were:

- He set up one form of prayers to be used before, during, and after the consecration of the bread and wine. Because these prayers were never to be changed, this part of the Eucharistic liturgy came to be called the *Canon,* which means *Rule* — that part of the Mass which should not be changed.
- He organized all the other prayers of the Eucharist around the Canon.
- He established Latin as the language of the Eucharist.
- He developed a special type of singing for the Eucharist. This music is still used and is called Gregorian chant, after Saint Gregory.

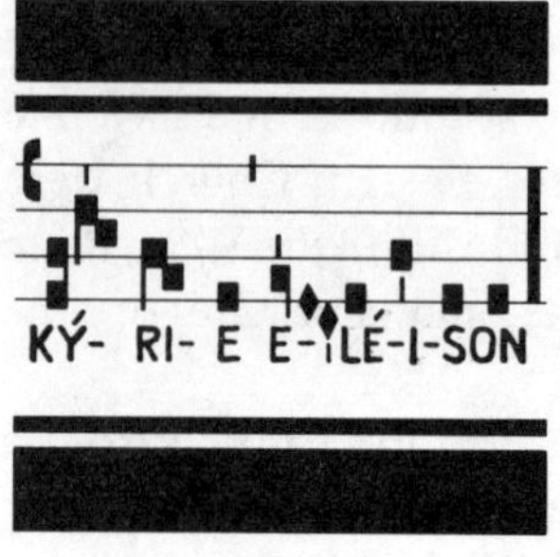

Gregory wanted to make sure that plain chant would be done well. He organized a boys' choir and was very proud of it. Even when he was in bed with rheumatism, he would gather the group for practice. He directed the singers with a stick that was long enough to discourage any fooling around.

From the time of Saint Gregory, the Eucharist was in many ways as it is today: a completely organized set of prayers and actions.

A Papal Mass

In Rome nothing equaled the splendor with which the pope surrounded the sacred liturgy. On a Sunday morning it was a common sight to see the pope mounted on horseback, accompanied by the entire Roman court, riding from his palace to the basilica where Mass was to be celebrated. With him rode the city officials since the pope was not only bishop of Rome but also the Roman governor.

A group of bishops and priests met the pope at the basilica. They welcomed him and led him to the sacristy, the room where he prepared for Mass. His rich vestments were a far cry from the poor garments of priests during the days of the persecution! Choir boys were there, too, robed in colorful gowns.

When all was ready, the pope made his majestic entry into the sanctuary. There, with prayers, readings, and chants, with bows, genuflections, and processions, the Mass began, moved forward, and continued to the end in solemn grandeur. It was truly a magnificent spectacle.

PART TWO

The Mass in the Middle Ages

(From A.D. 604 to A.D. 1517)

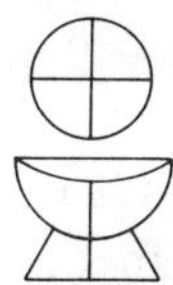

5

Charlemagne's Reform

Rome was governed by popes and other bishops for more than a century after Gregory the Great. But the city was still under the rule of the Eastern emperors, and popes often did not get along with emperors. Some emperors placed high taxes on Italy and made life hard for the popes. Unable to defend himself against these emperors, one pope — Leo III — asked for help from a leader named *Charlemagne*. Charlemagne — or Charles the Great — ruled Gaul, a vast territory northwest of Italy. Charlemagne agreed to help the pope. To show his thanks, Pope Leo III crowned Charlemagne as head of the Holy Roman Empire on Christmas Day in the year 800.

Charlemagne and Alcuin

Charlemagne was a great general. He protected his country, Gaul, from the attacks of the Saracens to the south and from the barbaric Saxons in the north. He likewise used his armies to protect the pope from a tribe of invading Lombards — Long Beards — that descended on Italy.

Charlemagne was also a religious man. As he moved from place to place in his campaigns, he attended Mass. It was then that he noticed, as Firmilian of Caesarea had once noticed nearly 600 years earlier, that no two churches in his empire celebrated Mass the same way. Except for the words of consecration, every priest celebrated Mass as he pleased. Charlemagne thought this was bad — bad for the unity of the Church, bad for the unity of his empire. He looked for ways to reform the liturgy.

During one of Charlemagne's trips to Italy, he met a Benedictine monk named Alcuin. Alcuin was on his way back from Rome to England, where he was director of the bishop's school at York. After Charlemagne talked with Alcuin, he felt that this English monk was just the man he needed to help in his liturgical reform. Charlemagne asked the bishop of York in England to let Alcuin live and work in Gaul for this purpose. The bishop was willing, and Alcuin came to live in Charlemagne's palace in Aachen.

Alcuin was pleased with this new appointment. For a long time he, too, had been thinking that the Mass should be celebrated in the same way everywhere. Now he saw that the only way of doing this was to take Mass as it was celebrated in Rome, Latin and all, and bring it north into Charlemagne's empire.

Charlemagne went along with Alcuin's suggestion. Still, Charlemagne knew that his people would never get used to the Roman Mass unless they could mix some of their own liturgical customs with it to give their Mass a "northern flavor."

Charlemagne sent personal messengers to Pope Adrian, asking him to send the exact wording of the Mass that he, the pope, celebrated.

This was asking a big favor. There were no printing presses at the time, and anything written had to be done by hand. It was a

The cathedral at Aachen built by Charlemagne

large task to write a whole book by hand, or even one week's Masses from beginning to end. But the pope needed Charlemagne's military protection too much to refuse him this service. The pope sent Charlemagne a book known as the *Hadrian Sacramentary.* This was Pope Adrian's collection of prayers for the Mass, baptisms, and other ceremonies.

Alcuin did not make many changes in Pope Adrian's prayers. The changes he made, he tested immediately in the emperor's chapel. The emperor attended these Masses, and after the Mass he discussed the new liturgy with Alcuin, with the priests assigned to the chapel, and with people who attended the services. Everyone had an opportunity to offer criticism and suggestions, and the new Mass was soon accepted.

Charlemagne's Changes

Charlemagne introduced his own changes into the new liturgy. Some of these he made on the spur of the moment, as the idea struck him.

One change had to do with the way people were called to Mass. The Romans used wooden clappers, two pieces of wood that clapped sharply against each other. In Gaul, Charlemagne preferred to use bells, and the louder they rang the better he liked it.

Another change was organ music. Rome did not allow any musical instruments in church. But when some friends of Charlemagne gave him an organ, he immediately installed it in his chapel. The people loved it.

In Rome, incense was considered a pagan perfume, and was rarely used at Mass. Charlemagne liked clouds of fragrant smoke, and used incense frequently.

At Alcuin's suggestion, Charlemagne also introduced the Spanish custom of praying the Nicene Creed during the Mass. However, he made his own rules about its use. Up to that time the Creed had been recited just before Communion. Charlemagne decided it should be sung. And he changed its place from before Communion to right after the Gospel — which is where we still have it today.

Success of the Reformed Liturgy

To make sure that his liturgical reform would be a success, Charlemagne decreed that the Eucharist must be celebrated his way throughout his empire. He appointed agents to see that the law was obeyed. The job these agents had was not very difficult. People in Gaul could see that the new Mass combined the advantages of the Roman Mass with the best from their own liturgy. With time, the reformed liturgy took such firm root that it continued even after Charlemagne's death.

This new liturgy became known as the *Gallo*-Roman Mass. It soon spread even outside Gaul. It was adopted and changed even further by the more northern Germanic countries. This further change was referred to as the *Germanic* Gallo-Roman Mass.

In the eleventh century, during times of danger, German emperors in the north often responded to calls for help from Italy and Rome in the south. Along with their barons and troops, these German rulers also brought their bishops and priests to Rome. And along with these priests came the *Germanic* Gallo-Roman liturgy. So now, the Mass that had left Rome had come back home — but with German changes in it. Rome took the Germanic liturgy, made some further changes, and then accepted it. Now it could be called the *Roman* Germanic-Gallo-Roman liturgy.

Eventually, this new Roman liturgy made its way back to the northern countries once again, where it stayed in use right up to the time of the Second Vatican Council in the 1960s. Many of its features were reforms made by Charlemagne.

6

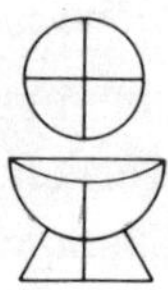

Suppression of Various Liturgies

As early as the late fourth century, and on through the ninth, popes had been trying to get the Roman liturgy adopted by the entire Western Church. But during all these centuries there was still much variety in the Eucharist. In some places individual priests celebrated Mass any way they pleased. Whole nations developed their own national liturgies. Two examples of national liturgies were the Celtic liturgy in Ireland and Brittany, and the Mozarabic liturgy in Spain.

Celtic Liturgy

Ireland was one place that had its own liturgy. Brittany, along the northwestern coast of France, was another. These two countries were the home of the Celtic people.

In the year 818, Emperor Louis the Pious of France fought with Brittany. The emperor won the battle and suppressed the Celtic liturgy, making the people of Brittany adopt the Roman liturgy.

Several centuries later, after a victory in 1172, England made the Irish Celts do the same.

There was nothing wrong with the Celtic liturgy. But the French emperor and the English king knew that if they allowed conquered people to keep their national liturgy, they would be leaving them an effective means of resisting government authority.

Mozarabic Liturgy

Another case of liturgical suppression was the *Mozarabic* liturgy.

Back in the eighth century, Arabs from Africa had invaded Spain. That invasion made communication between Spain and Rome very difficult. As a result, Spain had to organize its liturgical life more or less on its own. This was not difficult; for a long time Spain already had a liturgy well adapted to its culture. But cut off from Rome and influenced by Arab culture, Spain's liturgy became very wordy and elaborate — quite different from the clear, balanced Roman liturgy. The Mozarabic, or Spanish, liturgy continued until the eleventh century. Then Pope Gregory VII decided that Spain would be better off with the Roman liturgy. So the Mozarabic liturgy was no longer celebrated throughout Spain.

Should Liturgies Vary?

As head of the Church, Pope Gregory VII had the right to say which liturgies should be used. When he told Spain to do away with the Mozarabic liturgy, Gregory probably thought that unity in the liturgy would be a sign of unity in faith and a visible mark of that faith.

If Gregory were living now, after Vatican II, he might think differently. Popes today still require that certain parts in the Mass be the same everywhere. But the Church authority also encourages each nation to express its liturgy in its own cultural way. Once again we have unity in diversity, oneness with differences.

7

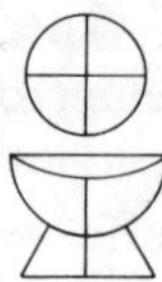

Gothic Liturgy

The years between A.D. 1014 and A.D. 1517 — the so-called Middle Ages — are sometimes spoken of as the "Gothic" period.

The word *Gothic* has different meanings for different people. Some hear the word and immediately think of the Goths, a race of barbarians who once overran the Roman Empire. Others think of it as a style of architecture which replaced classic Roman and Greek architecture. This last idea is closer to what *Gothic* means in this chapter.

The number of practicing Christians increased during the Gothic period, and larger churches were needed. This was especially noticeable on great feast days of the Church, when vast crowds came to celebrate Mass with their bishop.

Up to this time many of the churches had been built in the Greek-Roman style. These buildings were shaped like a rectangle or a shoe box, and had a flat or slightly tilted roof. The walls had to be strong to hold up the roof, and only small windows could be placed in them. Sometimes rows of pillars inside the buildings held part of the weight. Buildings constructed in this way could not be made large enough to hold thousands of people.

Gothic Architecture

To meet the need for larger churches, a new style of architecture came into use. We still call it the Gothic style. Its key feature was the pointed arch.

By using the arch, builders were able to make larger churches. Some of their buildings could hold 10,000 or more people. The sanctuary alone was often bigger than the large churches we see today.

These arches were reinforced and supported by "flying buttresses" — props built on the outside of the church. The arches and the props took the weight of the roof off the walls, so that large windows of stained glass could be placed in the walls.

The height of the building could also be increased. In some churches, the arched vault over the main altar rose to more than 150 feet! On the roof were steeples that doubled the height of the building. Everything about these churches pointed upward, so that the very buildings themselves seemed to be a prayer.

Cathedrals and the People Who Built Them

These huge churches were called cathedrals. The word *cathedral* comes from a Latin word that means "chair." In these spacious new churches a special thronelike chair was reserved for the bishop. (The cathedral is the bishop's church, the principal church of a diocese.)

After a bishop would decide to build a cathedral, the architects drew up their plans. Many played a part. Masons, stonecutters, sculptors, painters, and tapestry weavers gave of their talent. Thousands of volunteers put the stones into place by hand. One bishop described this army of volunteers:

"Powerful men, proud of their riches and accustomed to a life of ease, attached themselves with ropes to wagons and carted the stone, the lime, the wood, and other materials to where they were needed. Sometimes a thousand or more persons were necessary, so heavy was the load."

Builders at work on the abbey at St. Albans, England, in the mid-thirteenth century

The stonecutters formed the largest group. Day after day they cut and prepared the great stone blocks that would become the walls. Even during the long winter months when the weather delayed construction, these men worked on the stones. They did their work so well that when spring came the architects could take these stones just as they were and put them in place.

The stonecutters also sculptured marvelous statues and fantastic patterns of plants and animals to decorate doors, porches, and pillars. Some of these workers sculptured beautiful statues high on rooftops where only God could see them!

Another group were the artists who designed magnificent stained-glass windows. Some of these cathedral windows are 800 years old, and yet the colors in them are still fresh and bright. Modern artists have not yet discovered the secret of producing some of these colors. These windows show scenes from the life of the people who made them and illustrate stories from the Bible.

Weavers of fine cloth hung enormous, colorful wall banners called tapestries inside the cathedrals. Carpenters carved clever and amusing scenes on the paneling and woodwork in the apse, or sanctuary.

As a result of all this artistry, the cathedral itself was like a catechism for Gothic Christians. People who could not read learned great truths of their religion simply by studying the sculptures, tapestries, and stained-glass windows.

Completion of the Cathedrals

It took a hundred or more years to build some of the cathedrals. Notre Dame of Paris was begun in 1163 and completed in 1260. The cathedral at Chartres was started in the early twelfth century and was completed in the sixteenth century. It took that long to finish these buildings because of all the detail artists and sculptors put into them. In the cathedral at Chartres, for example, there are 3,889 figures in the stained-glass windows!

But what a joy, what a triumph, when the work was finished and the bishop led the first procession into his new cathedral. Bells would ring in the nearby belfries, announcing the event. People would come by the thousands, gathering under the great arched domes that seemed to reach all the way to heaven. There, in a splendor that our modern cathedrals have never equaled, the People of God would join with their bishop in celebrating the Mass.

The Gothic Period and the Mass

The Gothic period was an age of educational progress. The first European university, in Paris, was officially begun in the year 1215. Saints taught there — Albert the Great, Thomas Aquinas, and Bonaventure, to name only three. Thousands of students from all over Europe came to Paris and formed a "university world" as full of life and movement as that of any modern university. Christians began to study the learning and philosophies of the non-Christian Greeks and of the Muslims.

It was during this period that paper, which had been invented in China, was introduced into Europe by the Arabs. Paper was cheaper and more plentiful than the sheepskin parchment that Europeans still used. That made it available to more people, which also made communication easier.

The Gothic period was also an era of religious debate on many topics. Some of these arguments had to do with the presence of Christ in the Eucharist. For example, in the eleventh century a man named Berengar of Tours explained Christ's presence in the Eucharist in such a way that people thought he meant that maybe Christ is not really present. In the year 1079 a Council in Rome decided that Berengar's ideas were wrong. He and his followers were ordered to make a public confession of faith in the Eucharist. They also had to agree that only an ordained priest could celebrate Mass.

The people reacted to these doubts about the presence of Christ in the Eucharist by developing a great desire to *see* the consecrated Host as often as possible. The use of the *monstrance* — a showcase for the sacred Host — became popular, and there were many processions of the Blessed Sacrament. *Seeing* the Host became the "in" thing. Groups rushed from one church to another to see the Host when it was lifted up at the consecration. A bell would be rung to announce the consecration. For some people, the consecration was the only part of the Mass they attended. There is a documented story of a priest who would not raise the Host high enough to suit the people. They would shout to him, "Higher, Sir John, higher!"

The bishops were concerned about this attitude. In the year 1210, for example, the bishop of Paris told his priests not to lift up the unconsecrated bread at the Offertory of the Mass. The bishop did not want people to adore *bread* before it was even consecrated!

Monstrance

Strange as it may seem, during these years when people were so eager to see the consecrated Host, fewer and fewer people received communion. They seem to have forgotten that Christ is present in the Host mainly to be eaten as *food*. After all, the words of Jesus recorded in the Gospel of Saint Matthew are: "Take this and EAT it, this is my body."

Saint Thomas Aquinas

In every age, God has raised up great religious teachers. In the Middle Ages one of the greatest of these teachers was Saint Thomas Aquinas.

Thomas was born at Roccasecca, a little town near Naples, in 1225. He was the youngest son of Count Landulf of Aquino. As a six-year-old schoolboy with the Benedictines at Monte Cassino,

Thomas astonished his teachers by asking them, "What is God?" Later Thomas became a Dominican friar and studied at Cologne under the famous teacher Saint Albert the Great. In school Thomas spoke so little that his classmates called him a "dumb ox." But Albert the Great, who knew that Thomas was very intelligent, told the students: "Call him a dumb ox, if you will, but I tell you that his bellowings will shake the whole world."

After he began to preach and teach, Thomas wrote a long series of writings called *quaestiones disputatae* — religious questions that people were asking. Using the Bible and Church tradition, Thomas wrote answers that were easy to understand. Once when he had to answer a very difficult question, he went up to the altar and put his head against the tabernacle door. Then he said, "Lord, you know everything. You are present in this tabernacle. Give me the answer to this question."

Thomas wrote much about the Eucharist. He explained that this sacrament is the very heart of all the other sacraments. In the Mass, Thomas taught, Christ renews the sacrifice of Calvary and gives us Himself, His humanity and His divinity. Christ also remains in the Host even after the Mass is finished.

Developments in the Gothic Liturgy

Many developments in the liturgy during the Gothic period had to do with things related to the celebration of the Eucharist.

The *altar* became wider and longer. Up to that time, the altar had been scarcely a yard square in size. The enlarged altar was built of choice materials, decorated with enamel and sculptures. There was room on it for a crucifix, candles, and reliquaries (places where relics of saints are kept). In the center of the altar was a tabernacle where the Blessed Sacrament was kept. One bishop of Paris ordered: "The very sacred Body of Our Lord must be kept carefully and conscientiously in the most noble part of the altar under lock and key."

The *chalice* was the object of particular attention. In a church that was rich, the chalice had to be made of pure gold. If the church was poor, at least the cup part of the chalice had to be gold plate. Jewelers ornamented chalices with tiny sculptures, enamels, and even diamonds. The bishop had to bless the precious cups with sacred chrism (specially blessed oil).

During Mass the priest wore vestments that were made and blessed just for the liturgy. These robes had a stiff lining inside several layers of cloth. This made it possible for artists to paint and decorate the vestments. After a while these decorations became so important that the people spoke of the vestments as "liturgical ornaments."

Plain chant, the music of Saint Gregory the Great, became highly developed during this period. A Benedictine monk, Guy d'Arezzo, started using what we call the *do-re-mi* scale. In the abbey where Guy d'Arezzo lived, the monks began to chant in several voices. We still use a chant Mass that was composed at that time, the Mass of the Angels. Also at this time some of the Church's most beautiful Latin song verses were composed, such as the *Stabat Mater* and the *Pange Lingua*.

The book of *Holy Scripture* was given added marks of honor. It was solemnly carried during the Mass and incensed with respect as the Word of God. Monks made copies of the Scriptures and adorned the pages of their copies with brilliant colors. They drew fancy curlicues and tiny designs on the pages. This process was called *illuminating*.

Developments That Did Not Help

Gothic churches, with their beautiful art and music, helped people to appreciate the Eucharist. But there were also developments in this period that did not help. Here are three examples.

1. Priests began to celebrate most weekday Masses all by themselves with no other people present. This was not a good development because the Eucharist is basically a *community* celebration.

2. Also during this period, more and more people had Masses celebrated for their "special intentions." In itself, this is not a bad thing to do. But people began to have five, seven, even fifty Masses for the same intention. They thought that the more times you repeat the Mass, the better your chances are of getting your prayers answered. The important thing became numbers, not the Mass itself. That came very close to being superstition.

3. Also, during this period, priests were giving too much attention to gestures such as genuflecting, bowing, kissing the altar, holding one's arms in a certain position. There is nothing wrong with these gestures, but they were overdone. All this gesturing made the liturgy look more like a stage play than a prayer. The priest did most of this by himself while the people sat far away in the body of the church and had no real part in the Mass. All they did was watch the priest and his servers and listen to the choir.

Religious Drama

The Mass, with its yearly seasons of joy and sorrow, gave people ideas for other religious performances. People made up plays to celebrate Christmas, Easter, the lives of saints and martyrs, and above all the Passion of Christ. Some of these plays were like the world-famous Passion Play that began in the seventeenth century and takes place every year in the lovely German village of Oberammergau.

Crowds enjoyed these plays so much that they had them repeated time and again. They sat for hours listening and watching until they knew the plays by heart. They laughed until they cried when they heard the donkey giving the prophet Balaam a rough time (a story in the Old Testament Book of Numbers). When they saw the little man Zacchaeus climbing a tree to see Jesus, they cheered if the actor got up the tree very nimbly, and booed if he was clumsy. They shed real tears as they silently followed the long Passion of Christ.

Pilgrimages

The people liked to watch plays about Christ and the saints. Many of them also wanted to visit the Holy Land or see the shrines of saints. In the Middle Ages incredible numbers of pilgrims set out in long caravans, even though the roads were terrible and the countryside was full of bandits. Every year a half million went to Saint James of Compostella in Spain. Two million pilgrims appeared in Rome for the first Jubilee, and there were never fewer than 200,000 pilgrims at a time in the city. Hundreds of thousands went to Jerusalem. In the year 1604, the bishop of Bamber led 7,000 pilgrims to this holy city. And always, at the end of the pilgrimage, there was Mass with Communion.

Conclusion

Some modern artists and scholars think that the Gothic age was a glorious time in history. Others disagree. Apart from what anyone says about the Gothic period, the Mass was at the heart of Christian life at that time. Remember that:

The Eucharist began the people's Sunday and set the rhythm for their week.

The great liturgical feasts with their solemn Masses marked the seasons of the year with celebrations of events in the life of Christ and the saints.

The famous cathedrals were built around the altar for the celebration of the Eucharist.

The Eucharist was the final event of pilgrimages which drew thousands of Christians onto the road to shrines and holy places.

From the Eucharist grew the religious plays and dramas.

The Eucharist inspired the most beautiful chants of the period and encouraged musical art.

PART THREE

The Mass in Modern Times

(From A.D. 1517 to Today)

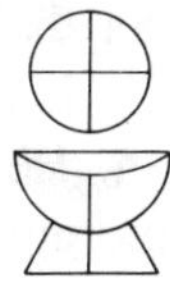

8

Martin Luther and Liturgical Change

In the year 1517, an Augustinian priest named Martin Luther started a movement known as the Protestant Reformation. Martin Luther said that many things in the Church needed to be changed because they were wrong. Some of the things Luther wanted to change had to do with the Mass. The pope ordered Luther to stop speaking out, but Luther refused. He and his followers went their own way and eventually became the Lutheran Church.

Today, over 450 years later, Catholics and Lutherans are discovering how close they really are in matters of faith and worship. Today there is Christian love between the two Churches. But in those days there was a lot of confusion and fighting.

Martin Luther

Martin Luther was born in 1483 into a German farm family. His parents were very strict with him. They were determined that Martin should make something of himself, so they sent him to school. The schoolmaster was so strict that he once gave Martin fifteen spankings in a single day.

One of the earliest woodcut portraits of Martin Luther, probably drawn in 1520

When Martin was fifteen, he went to live with an uncle. This uncle also was a hard man. He often made Martin study for long hours without anything to eat.

As soon as Martin Luther was old enough, he attended the great German university at Erfurt. It was at this time that he had several painful experiences. First, a good friend of his died suddenly. Next, a contagious disease spread throughout the university city and caused many deaths. Finally, Martin himself was caught in a thunderstorm and knocked down by a lightning bolt. Sixteen days after the shock of the thunderstorm, Martin entered the Augustinian monastery in Erfurt. It was the year 1505. Two years later he was ordained a priest and celebrated his first Mass on April 4, 1507.

Luther's New Idea

As a young monk, Martin Luther worried about his sins, afraid he would go to hell. Because his father had been rough with him, Martin had fearful ideas of God the Father. One night while Martin was worrying, the idea suddenly came to him that it is wrong to think we can earn our salvation by what we do. All that is necessary is to have faith in Jesus.

Martin Luther began telling other people his idea. At first not many people listened. Then, in 1517, ten years after Luther became a priest, a Dominican friar named Johann Tetzel came to Germany. Tetzel preached in the churches and asked for donations to help build Saint Peter's Basilica in Rome. Tetzel told the people that if they gave a donation, they could get their dead relatives and friends out of purgatory and into heaven. From what Tetzel said, people got the idea that they could buy their way into heaven if they had enough money.

When Luther heard this strange doctrine, he began to preach against it. Luther also wrote a long list of statements — his famous Ninety-five Theses — and nailed them onto the doors of the castle church in the city of Wittenberg.

Luther's Ninety-five Theses became famous. Soon, in Germany and in other places in Europe, people began to take sides. The pope read the Ninety-five Theses and told Luther to take back the ones that were against Church teaching. When Luther refused, the pope excommunicated him — put him out of the Church.

Luther's Example Spreads

Now Luther and a friend named Philip Melancthon organized a new form of worship to take the place of the Roman Mass. Luther did away with Latin; he used the language of the people in his new prayer service. As a result, every Lutheran church became a national church — German in Germany, Swedish in Sweden, Danish in Denmark.

Luther's example of separating himself from the Catholic Church was followed by others. In 1533 a man named John Calvin became dissatisfied with the Church. He, too, thought some Catholic doctrines needed reform. He broke away and began his own church in Switzerland. His followers were called Calvinists.

A year after Calvin's breakaway, King Henry VIII of England started the Anglican Church, the Church of England. Henry's split with the Catholic Church had nothing to do with reform. He was angry with the pope for not allowing him to divorce his wife and marry another woman.

So it was that within twenty years Luther, Calvin, and Henry VIII had caused a breakup in the Catholic liturgy.

Spread of the Various Forms of Worship

For Europe, the sixteenth century was an age of discovery and exploration. It was also a time of colonization and missionary activity. Wherever the colonists settled, the missionaries were among them. Besides Catholic missionaries, there were also Lutherans, Calvinists, and Anglicans.

Lutheranism. In its early days, Lutheranism was limited more or less to countries that speak German. These countries were not interested in colonization, so there was little growth of Lutheranism outside Europe. Gradually, however, Lutheranism spread from its German homeland into other countries. Today there are many Lutherans in the United States and Canada.

Anglicanism. England was greatly interested in colonization. For a long time, however, the English seldom passed their Anglican religion on to the natives of the countries they colonized. But that is no longer true. The Anglican Church, like other religious groups, has many missionaries outside England.

Calvinism. In the Church of England there was a group of people who decided that Anglican worship was still too Catholic. To change this, they adopted Calvin's ideas into their religious belief. Because they wanted to "purify" the Church of England, these English Calvinists were called *Puritans*.

The queens and kings who headed the Church of England wanted the Puritans to accept Anglicanism just as it was. The Puritans refused. A small group of them left England and fled to Holland, where they could worship God as they pleased. Later, some of these Puritans and another group from England embarked on the Mayflower and sailed to America. They planned to settle in Virginia, but storms drove their ship farther north. On December 21, 1620, they landed at Plymouth Rock in the Cape Cod region of New England. This is how Calvinism came to the northeastern United States.

Catholicism. The Catholic Church also took advantage of the colonization that was going on in the sixteenth century. Catholic missionaries sailed along with Spanish explorers to the New World, America. Soon Catholicism was firmly planted in all of South and Central America. Later, from Mexico it spread to the West Coast of North America. California's largest cities are reminders of the early presence of Catholic missionaries; they have names such as San Diego (Saint James), Los Angeles (The Angels), and San Francisco (Saint Francis).

In the northeastern part of North America, the large Canadian province of Quebec became Catholic because of French missionaries who traveled with the explorers sent by the kings of France. Some of these missionaries gave their lives as martyrs for the Christian faith. Because of their work and sacrifices, Quebec today is eighty-five percent Catholic.

Missionaries also accompanied Portuguese explorers to India. In India the Catholic Church took strong hold in the province of Goa. One of the missionaries who went to India was the Jesuit priest, Saint Francis Xavier. After preaching to the people of Goa, Saint Francis Xavier set out for China, but he died before he reached the Chinese mainland. The story of how later missionaries introduced Christianity into China will be told in the next chapter.

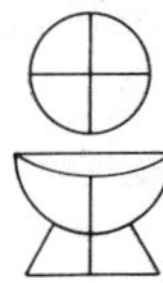

9

Reform of the Catholic Liturgy

In Martin Luther's time the Church needed reform. Many Catholics, including priests and monks and nuns, were not living serious Christian lives.

In order to correct these abuses, the pope and the bishops of the Catholic Church decided to have an ecumenical council. The great meeting began at Trent, a little town in northeast Italy, in the year 1545. During its twenty-five meetings, the members of the Council laid down rules to correct problems in the Church. Because Martin Luther had challenged many Church teachings, including teachings about the Mass, the bishops spent much time discussing the liturgy and the Eucharist. Here are some of the teachings the bishops agreed on at the Council of Trent:

— Christ remains in the consecrated Host even after Mass is over. So it is proper to have processions of the Blessed Sacrament and to adore Christ in the consecrated Host.

— Christ is totally present under the form of bread and also under the form of wine. So, if a person receives Christ only under one form, bread or wine, that person receives Jesus in Communion.

— Mass may be offered for the living and for the dead.

— Christ ordained priests to offer his body and blood, so only an ordained priest has the power to offer the Mass.

The Council of Trent began in the year 1545. It lasted eighteen years, and ended in 1563.

The Roman Missal of Pope Saint Pius V

At the Council of Trent the bishops had wanted to reform the liturgy. But they realized that this work could take years, and the Council had already gone on too long. So they decided to have the pope take care of liturgical reform after the Council was over.

Within years after the Council of Trent, Pope Pius V had the new Roman liturgy ready. Every Catholic bishop and priest in the world had to follow the new liturgy of Trent. This liturgy was in Latin, and no one was permitted to change it into any other language. "Let no one change anything!" warned the pope.

For the next four hundred years — until the Second Vatican Council — the liturgy of Trent from Pope Pius V was used in the Catholic Church. It told the priest exactly *how* he was to celebrate Mass; how far apart to hold his hands at certain prayers, how deeply to bow, when he was to kiss the altar and the book of the Gospel, and on and on. All these directions were printed right in the priest's missal.

The Mass of Pope Pius V was good news in several ways. In churches where false teachings had crept into the Mass, the new liturgy was an improvement. It also brought order to churches where the liturgy had become disorganized.

But the new liturgy also reinforced some negative features. For example, it allowed the Mass to be celebrated only in Latin. The problem with Latin was that most people did not know it. As a result, people could not really take part in the Mass. All they could do was watch the priest and hear him say words they did not understand. What people did was called "hearing" Mass.

Another regulation was that people had to fast from all food and drink from midnight until after going to Communion just as the priest had to do. And at high Masses and funeral Masses the people were not permitted to receive Holy Communion. Because of these regulations fewer people received Communion.

The Mass in China

Martin Luther had his public prayer services in the language of the people. However, Pope Saint Pius V said the Mass *must* be celebrated in Latin. At the time, no one realized the effect this policy would have on the Church, especially in China.

For hundreds of years China had been closed to Catholic missionaries. During the 1850s a Jesuit priest named Matteo Ricci finally got into the country. Because he knew that the Chinese admired educated people, Matteo Ricci came to China as a scholar, dressed in silken robes like a university professor. He presented himself at the emperor's court, where everyone was astonished at Ricci's knowledge of astronomy and geography. The emperor himself was so pleased that he gave the Jesuits permission to enter China as missionaries.

Matteo Ricci, S.J.

In 1610 when Matteo Ricci died, other educated Jesuits continued his work. Within a few years there were 150,000 Catholic converts, many in the emperor's own family. Some young Chinese men became priests.

When the Jesuits saw how many Chinese people were becoming Catholics, they asked Pope Paul V to give them permission to celebrate liturgy in the Chinese language. The pope agreed.

A Quarrel Breaks Out

For a long time the Jesuits were the only Catholic missionaries working in China. Then other missionary groups came. Among these new missionaries, many did not understand the ways of the Chinese people nor the methods of the Jesuits. Instead of accepting Chinese customs, some of the new missionaries considered everything Chinese as pagan idolatry. Since the liturgy was in Chinese, they were sure there was idolatry in the Mass, too.

One missionary, a Spanish Dominican who had been put out of one other country and then out of China, went to Rome and complained about the Jesuits. The Jesuits heard of this and sent one of their own men to Rome. In Rome, the Jesuit explained that missionaries had been celebrating the Eucharist in Chinese for a hundred years. There was no idolatry in it. But Pope Clement XI began to think it had been a mistake for Pope Paul V to have allowed the Mass in Chinese. The pope ordered all missionaries to start celebrating the Mass in Latin again. Even worse, the prayers the Chinese people said during Mass were no longer allowed to be the same prayers the priest said at the altar.

The Jesuits obeyed the pope, but they were afraid that their success at winning the Chinese to Christ would end. They were right. The Chinese emperors, who had been friendly toward the Church, became furious. For almost two centuries they imprisoned and put to death hundreds of bishops, priests, and religious men and women. In spite of all this, the Catholic faith remained rooted in China, and it is still there today.

Looking Back to the Council of Trent

The Council of Trent did many good things. It put an end to some abuses. It explained clearly what the Church taught, and stirred up Christian devotion to the Eucharist.

As centuries went on, critics found fault with the liturgy of Trent, especially the Roman Missal. Everything in it was "frozen" in the same form it had in the sixteenth century, said the critics.

Little by little the popes themselves began to see that this was true. Over the years they changed some of the old strict rules of Pope Pius V. In 1898 a translation of the Mass prayers was officially permitted. In our own century Pope Pius X urged the people to receive Holy Communion daily, and in 1910 he permitted little children to receive the Eucharist.

When John XXIII became pope in 1958, he sent out a new set of rules for the Mass. Shortly afterwards he announced a new Council, Vatican II. Just as Pope Pius V had done after the Council of Trent, the Second Vatican Council revised the Roman Missal and gave the Church the liturgy we have today.

10

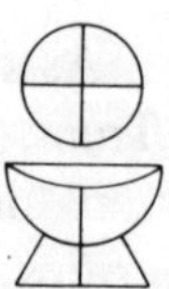

The Eucharist of Vatican II

John XXIII was elected pope on October 28, 1958, when he was almost seventy-seven years old. Many people said he would not last long enough to do anything. If Pope John heard that, he must have smiled to himself. John had been pope less than a month when he told his secretary, "We need a council." Two months later, he said the same thing to the Church cardinals who were his advisors. This was not a sudden idea that Pope John had. Even before he was elected pope, he had thought that a council was needed. Still, the cardinals could not believe the pope was serious. *Who wanted a council?* the cardinals asked themselves. *Who needed one?* One day a visitor asked John outright, "Why a council?" Instead of answering immediately, Pope John rose from his chair, walked over to the window and opened it wide. Then, turning back to his visitor, he said, "Why a council? Just for this — to let some fresh air come into the Church."

The Second Vatican Council

On October 11, 1962, the Council met for the first time. More than 2,000 cardinals and bishops were present. There were also ambassadors from various countries, representatives of international organizations, and delegates from other Churches.

The Council was held in the Basilica of Saint Peter in Vatican City. Because another council had already met in the same place years before, this new one became the *Second* Vatican Council.

Pope John personally opened the Council in 1962, but he was not there when it closed in December 1965. He died on June 3, 1963, and a new pope — Paul VI — carried on the Council. It is to Pope Paul VI that we owe the liturgical reforms that began in the 1960s.

Popes Paul VI (top), John Paul II (left), and John XXIII

The Liturgy of Vatican II

Liturgy was the first item of business at the Council. After nearly a year of hard work, the Council bishops approved the final document. It was called the *Constitution on the Sacred Liturgy,* and was published by Pope Paul VI on December 4, 1963.

This document says that liturgy is very important in the life of the Church and that we need to revise and adapt our liturgy to the needs of people today.

The key word in the Liturgy Constitution is *participation*. The liturgy is "an *action of Christ the Priest and of His Body which is the Church*," this document states. Liturgy is not something that we sit and watch the priest do. It is something *we do with Christ*.

One of the major reforms in our liturgy has been the change to the language of the people. The Last Supper was in Aramaic, the language of Jesus and the Apostles. In the third century, when the Roman liturgy was in Greek, Pope Callistus changed it to Latin because that was the language most Romans understood. Now, in our own time, the liturgy is once again in the language of the people. If you go to Mass in Paris or Tokyo, you will see Catholics joining right in with the priest because they know what they are saying and singing. The language change makes it possible to have full *participation*.

Sunday Mass Before and After Vatican II

There are Catholics today who have never seen the "old" liturgy we had before Vatican II. To show how much things have changed, let us imagine an American anthropologist who went to live with a tribe of Indians in the tropical rain forests of Brazil. Living out of touch with civilization, the anthropologist, Dr. Malcolm Boileau, had no idea what was happening in the Catholic Church during the 1960s, 1970s, and 1980s. Now he has returned home to New Orleans, and his brother, Warren Boileau, takes him to Sunday Mass.

* * *

Warren and Malcolm enter the parish church. The first thing Malcolm notices is that there are two altars up in front. There is the altar he remembers, the one attached to the woodwork of the sanctuary, with steps leading up to it. But then there is another altar down lower, nearer to the pews where the people are.

"Why two altars?" Malcolm whispers to Warren.

"Because our old altar couldn't be moved out," says Warren. "The newer churches have only the one altar. It's closer to the people so they can see the priest and hear what he says. It makes it easier for them to take part in the Mass. You'll see when the priest starts."

They kneel. "I forgot to bring my old missal," Malcolm mutters.

"You don't need it," says Warren. He hands Malcolm a missalette.

Malcolm pages through the booklet. He leans toward Warren. "What's happened to the Latin? You mean the Mass is in English?"

Warren smiles. "In English, in German, in Polish, whatever language the people speak."

Malcolm shakes his head. Just then the priest enters the sanctuary. He goes to the altar, kisses it, and immediately goes to his chair.

Malcolm remembers the kissing of the altar, but the priest's going to the chair is something new. Before Vatican II the priest went up to the altar, kissed it, then came down the altar steps, said the *Confiteor* — a confession of sinfulness — and went back up to the altar.

From his chair the priest greets the people. But there is no Latin greeting, no *Dominus vobiscum* (The Lord be with you). Everything is in English. Later, Malcolm will discover that the priest's informal greeting may change from week to week and even from Mass to Mass. There are also several different forms of penitential prayers that follow, prayers about our sinfulness, and the priest may choose whichever seems to fit best.

While Malcolm is taking all of this in, the priest says the prayer of the day. Afterwards, the priest sits, and a young woman goes and stands at the lectern, where she begins reading from the Old Testament.

Malcolm can hardly believe his eyes. Back in the 1950s, only a deacon or a subdeacon could take the priest's place for that reading. Now pastors can appoint lay people to be lectors.

When the first reading is finished, another woman walks to the lectern and reads from the New Testament. This second reading comes as a surprise to Malcolm. There used to be only one reading before the Gospel; now there are two.

After the homily, the people keep standing for the Prayers of the Faithful. Malcolm listens to the petitions.

"Why are we doing this?" Malcolm asks Warren.

"The early Christians used to offer prayers like this," says Warren. "Later the prayers were dropped from the Mass. Vatican II put them in again."

Malcolm listens, but already he is distracted by what he sees. A family is bringing the offerings of bread and wine to the priest at the altar. The ushers, too, are bringing the collection baskets, bringing them before the altar.

Malcolm watches as the priest takes the bread and wine, stands behind the altar, and faces the people. The priest is saying the Mass prayers aloud. At times the people answer.

As the Mass continues, Malcolm notices in his missalette that there are several Eucharistic Prayers. There used to be only one such prayer, and it was called the *Canon,* meaning Rule. In the old days the priest recited the Canon in such a low tone that no one could hear him. Now the priest prays even the sacred words of the consecration aloud! Malcolm learns later that there are Eucharistic Prayers for children's Masses, too, and for special feasts.

Everyone rises to say the *Our Father* with the priest. Now Malcolm is in for a shock. The priest invites: *"Let us offer each other the sign of peace."* And right there in church, with Jesus

present on the altar, people turn to each other and smile, shake hands, and hug. Malcolm is still in shock when Warren clasps his hand.

"What's the matter?" Warren asks.

"I don't get it. What's with this 'sign of peace'?"

Warren smiles. "You'll get used to it, Malcolm. It's a sign of Christian love. The Peace of Christ to you, old friend!"

Communion time comes. Malcolm is suddenly uneasy. He had not noticed before, but there is no communion rail to kneel at. He waits and watches people standing as the priest places the host on their tongues — *or in their hands!*

He nudges Warren sharply. *"In the hand?"*

"Right," whispers Warren. "Like the early Christians. And you may receive the Precious Blood if you want to."

Warren and Malcolm walk toward the altar. Malcolm sees now that the priest is not the only person distributing Holy Communion. Men and women dressed in their regular Sunday clothes are also giving out Communion.

Malcolm is aware that a great number of people are receiving Communion. This is an eleven o'clock Mass. Back in the 1950s, at an eleven o'clock Mass, sometimes Communion was not even distributed. The long fast from midnight made Communion that late almost impossible. But Warren has told Malcolm that now the fast is only for an hour before receiving the Sacrament.

After Communion the priest and people remain seated for a few minutes. It is a time of silent thanksgiving. Finally, the priest rises, recites a prayer, gives the blessing and says: *Go in peace to love and serve the Lord*.

As the two leave the church, Warren turns to Malcolm. "How'd you like it?"

"Well, it's different. I'll have to get used to it. But I like it. Somehow I feel as if I've been to Mass for the first time in my life. I felt like I was really part of it."

"That's it," said Warren. "You're part of it."

Conclusion

In the entire history of the Mass there has never been a reform like the one made by Vatican II. There were changes made in the past, but never anything so complete and in so short a time. This has been a sharp "hairpin turn" back toward the Mass as it used to be said in the time of the early Christians.

Thanks to Vatican II and Pope Paul VI, we have a new liturgy today. But with all the changes, what we have is truly the Mass of Christ. What has changed is the manner of its celebration, the liturgy. For there can never be a new Mass. At its heart, the Eucharist is the same yesterday, today, and forever.

CHAPTER VIII.

WHAT MUST AN HONEST CHRISTIAN DO ABOUT BAPTISM?

There are three courses which a man may follow in regard to baptism.

1. FOLLOW CATHOLICS IN CHANGING BAPTISM AS TO MODE AND MEANING.

2. FOLLOW MODERNISTS IN LEAVING OFF BAPTISM.

3. FOLLOW THE BIBLE AND BE BAPTIZED THE BIBLE WAY.

If he believes, as Catholics do, that the church has a right to change what God plainly commanded, that it does not especially matter any way, then he can accept the Catholic's substitute for baptism as many modern denominations have done. It is very likely that he will find himself accepting a lot of Catholic doctrine as well. Certainly he will miss the plain Bible meaning of baptism.

If a man seeks to please people instead of God, he may ignore the repeated commands of the Saviour Himself, and of the Scriptures, ignore the example of New Testament Christians, and do away with baptism as has Dr. Harry Emerson Fosdick and Dr. Shailer Mathews and other modernists and so many so-called "community churches." Such a person will be counted very broad-minded and very liberal, but he will be untrue to the Bible and disobedient to Jesus Christ.

Some people are so disgusted with denominationalism, especially those denominations patterned after Rome (and well they might be!) that they like to do away with every requirement that reminds them of their past bondage. Community churches usually commit the very foolish mistake of trying to please everybody. They sometimes offer to baptize people "any way that suits you best," like the school teacher who proposed to the trustees of a rural school that he would teach the world was flat or round, just as they preferred! In some cases, such churches prefer not to take a positive stand on any matter of Bible doctrine about which there is controversy.

CONTENTS

sions and teach people to disobey the Bible's plain commands, the teachers and preachers and theologians of all the centuries since Christ have agreed on this matter, that baptism is for this age of grace. You will agree, too, that baptism is for you, for all Christians in this age, I feel sure, if you will with a teachable, humble heart, search the Scriptures with us here.

BAPTISM, AS COMMANDED IN THE GREAT COMMISSION, IS TO "ALL NATIONS," AND "TO THE END OF THE WORLD"

Study this Great Commission as given in Matthew 28:18-20:

> **"And Jesus came and spake unto them, saying, All power is given unto me in heaven and in earth. Go ye therefore, and teach all nations, baptizing them in the name of the Father, and of the Son, and of the Holy Ghost: Teaching them to observe all things whatsoever I have commanded you: and, lo, I am with you alway, even unto the end of the world. Amen."**

This Commission was given on the authority of Jesus Christ over Heaven and earth. Then certainly it was not merely local. This Great Commission, including baptism, was commanded to ALL NATIONS. That included others besides Jews. Jesus closed the command with a promise. "Lo, I am with you alway, even unto the end of the world," which shows that the command was not given merely to those apostles, but to other Christians lasting down to the end of the world. It is clear that Jesus spoke to these men, not as to Jews, but as to apostles responsible for setting up churches and giving the doctrines for this Christian dispensation. It is foolish to teach that this was for Jews only.

In Acts 2:38, 39, Peter, speaking to the Jews at Pentecost, commanded them to repent and be baptized, telling them that they should receive the gift of the Holy Ghost. But in verse 39 he plainly taught them that the same promise of the gift of the Holy Ghost to those who repented and were baptized is for all people everywhere. His words are:

> **"For the promise is unto you, and to your children, and to all that are afar off, even as many as the Lord our God shall call."**

Baptism is for all that are afar off, as many as God calls.

GENTILES WERE BAPTIZED AS WELL AS JEWS

Remember that the ministry to the Gentiles began immediately after Pentecost, and we have full detailed record of that in the New Testament. In fact, every book in the New Testament was written after the gospel was being preached regularly, far and wide, to the Gentiles. That particular ministry to the Gentiles was begun by Peter under direct command of God in the tenth chapter of Acts. The Lord especially taught and prepared Peter for that ministry and showed him that the ceremonial law concerning Gentiles was now done away and that what God had cleansed, he was not to call common as Jews had done heretofore. Peter went and preached to the house of Cornelius the gospel of salvation by faith (Acts 10:34-48). Peter began his sermon with the statement that in God's sight there is no difference between Jew and Gentile (vss. 34, 35). When Cornelius and his household were converted, Peter spoke to the six brethren who were with him, showing that **these Gentiles should be baptized,** just as the Jews were, since they had the same Holy Spirit. Then we are told:

> **"And he commanded them to be baptized in the name of the Lord."** (vs. 48).

There is no difference there between Jews and Gentiles. Gentiles were baptized as well as Jews, when they were saved.

PAUL CAME NOT TO BAPTIZE BUT HE BAPTIZED AND TAUGHT BAPTISM

Paul was an apostle to the Gentiles. That was true from the very first as you see from Acts 9:15 where at the conversion of Paul the Lord told Ananias, "For he is a chosen vessel unto me, to bear my name before the Gentiles." In Galatians 2:7 Paul says, "The gospel of the uncircumcision was committed unto me, as the gospel of the circumcision was unto Peter." Paul tells us that when he first came back to Jerusalem after his conversion the Lord told him in Acts 22:21:

> **"And he said unto me, Depart: for I will send thee far hence unto the Gentiles."**

But Paul, the apostle to the Gentiles, everywhere preached and practiced baptism, of Gentiles as well as Jews! Either Paul or Silas, or both, baptized the jailer and his family, the same hour of the night, when they were converted at Philippi (**Acts 16:33**). **Lydia was**

likewise baptized (Acts 16:15), and Crispus (Acts 18:8). Paul taught the people everywhere he went to be baptized, and even in some cases baptized the converts himself, though he did not want people to think that it was any better to be baptized with his own hands than by anybody else.

Baptism was never the principal matter with Paul, as it ought not to be with any preacher. In I Corinthians 1:17 Paul said:

> **"For Christ sent me not to baptize, but to preach the gospel."**

Some opponents of baptism try to prove by this Scripture that Paul did not believe in baptism. The very opposite is true, as you see when you read the entire passage, (I Corinthians 1:11-17):

> **11. "For it hath been declared unto me of you, my brethren, by them which are of the house of Chloe, that there are contentions among you. 12. Now this I say, that every one of you saith, I am of Paul; and I of Apollos; and I of Cephas; and I of Christ. 13. Is Christ divided? was Paul crucified for you? or were ye baptized in the name of Paul? 14. I thank God that I baptized none of you, but Crispus and Gaius; 15. Lest any should say that I had baptized in mine own name. 16. And I baptized also the household of Stephanas: besides, I know not whether I baptized any other. 17. For Christ sent me not to baptize, but to preach the gospel: not with wisdom of words, lest the cross of Christ should be made of none effect."**

The church of Corinth had contentions among them as you see in verses 11 and 12. Some people boasted that they were following Paul, that Paul baptized them. Others favored Apollos. Others claimed to follow Peter. Paul replied that he baptized only a few of them with his own hands, and was glad that he did not baptize others, but had others do the baptizing, since people would make it a matter of contention. That is, evidently, the same reason that Jesus did not baptize anybody with His own hands but had His disciples baptize many, as you see in John 4:1, 2. In verse 13 Paul reminds them that it was Christ who was crucified for them, and that they were baptized in the name of Christ, not in the name of Paul. Then Paul told these quarreling Christians that it was not his business to baptize somebody to be a follower of himself, but that he came to preach the gospel. Paul did not mean that God did not intend for him to baptize people, or to write letters to Christians, or to teach young preachers who went with him. He did all of these things and taught others to

do them, but his mission was to preach the gospel and get people saved! John the Baptist "came for a witness, to bear witness of the LIGHT" (John 1:6-8). Yet John baptized, as God had commanded him to do. Jesus Himself "came into the world to save sinners" (I Timothy 1:15), but we are plainly told that through His disciples He baptized multitudes (John 3:23, and John 4:1). Jesus gave the commission to his disciples "to preach the gospel to every creature"; but, in the same command, He plainly told them to baptize the converts! Baptism does not save people and is not as important as getting people saved; but it is important enough that every Christian ought to receive it, because Jesus commanded it.

When you study the inspired statement of Paul, as quoted above in I Corinthians 1:11-17, you will see several clear facts concerning baptism:

(1) Paul had taught the people at Corinth to be baptized. He referred to baptism several times in this letter.

(2) They had been baptized in the name of Christ, not in the name of Paul (verse 13).

(3) Paul had baptized some of them with his own hands.

(4) The only reason Paul would not have gladly baptized all of them was "lest any should say that I had baptized in mine own name" (verse 15).

PAUL PREACHED AND PRACTICED BAPTISM EVERYWHERE

In his letters to the Christians at Corinth, at Rome, at Colosse, at Ephesus, and to the churches of Galatia, Paul discussed baptism in every case, and the converts at those places were baptized. In fact, Paul went into detail to remind them again of the meaning of baptism in Colossians 2:12 and Romans 6:3-5. It is foolish to pretend that baptism meant in those cases anything different from what it meant in the Great Commission, and in the teaching and example of Jesus Himself. Remember also that the word **baptism** in the Bible always means baptism with water unless the passage plainly teaches otherwise. The word **baptism** never refers to the baptism of the Holy Ghost in the Bible unless it says so. The literal meaning of baptism is with water, and that is true throughout the New Testament as you will immediately see when you look through the concordance and read every passage which mentions baptism. All these Gentiles, then,

converted through Paul's ministry, were taught baptism and were baptized with water. Paul referred freely to baptism when he wrote to them in Colossians 2:12, Romans 6:3-5, I Corinthians 1:13, Galations 3:27 and Ephesians 4:5.

Peter, also, in his epistles "to the strangers scattered throughout Pontus, Galatia, Cappadocia, Asia, and Bithynia," who were converted, reminded them of their baptism and gives the meaning of baptism as "the answer of a good conscience toward God," and says that it is a figure of the resurrection of Jesus Christ. Read the following passage in I Peter 3:20, 21:

> **"... the ark ... wherein few, that is, eight souls were saved by water. The like figure whereunto even baptism doth also now save us (not the putting away of the filth of the flesh, but the answer of a good conscience toward God,) by the resurrection of Jesus Christ."**

This passage clearly refers to water baptism, a figure of the resurrection of Jesus, and was addressed to converts in many nations, and this was written long after Pentecost. Honest people who believe the Bible must conclude that baptism was for Gentiles as well as Jews, and that the command is given to every Christian to the end of this age.

BAPTISM NOT ONE OF THE "ORDINANCES" NAILED TO THE CROSS

Some people quote Colossians 2:14 as a command against baptism. That verse says:

> **"Blotting out the handwriting of ordinances that was against us, which was contrary to us, and took it out of the way, nailing it to his cross."**

Because baptism and the Lord's Supper are commonly called "ordinances," then ignorant people say that these were done away with at the death of Christ. However, when you read that chapter, it becomes obvious that the ordinances mentioned are the Old Testament ceremonial laws which verse 17 says "are a shadow of things to come, but the body is of Christ." The death of Christ on the cross certainly did not blot out His instruction about baptism, for the Great Commission, commanding the disciples to baptize, was given after the crucifixion and resurrection of Christ! All the books of the

New Testament, mentioning baptism scores of times, were written after the resurrection of Jesus! In fact, just two verses above Colossians 2:14, in verse 12, Paul has just stated that baptism was a picture of the new life which Christians, being free from the ceremonial law, had by faith in Christ.

Acts 28:28 where Paul said to the Jews in Rome, "Be it known therefore unto you, that the salvation of God is sent unto the Gentiles, and that they will hear it," is sometimes used as an argument that after that time the order of things changed and that baptism was done away with. How foolish! In the first place, that Scripture says nothing about changing baptism; and in the second place, the same thing had happened a number of other times with Jews in other places. For instance in Acts 13:46, Paul and Barnabas preached the gospel to the Jews at Antioch in Pisidia. When these Jews rejected the gospel, as did the Jews at Rome in Acts 28:25-28, Paul said to them the same thing that he later said to the Jews at Rome: "But seeing ye put it from you, and judge yourselves unworthy of everlasting life, lo, we turn to the Gentiles." In fact, when you compare Acts 28:25-28 with Matthew 13:10-17, you will see that Jesus said the same thing as Paul did, and quoted identically the same Old Testament Scripture about the Jews, even before His crucifixion! The Jews as a nation had rejected Christ before His crucifixion. When Paul carried the gospel to the various towns, the same thing happened everywhere he went. But he went on preaching the same gospel to Jews and Gentiles, and the converts were baptized just as Jesus commanded in the Great Commission.

It is clear to all who are willing to take God's Word for it that baptism is for this generation the same as in Bible times and is commanded for Gentiles the same as for Jews.

NO NEW DISPENSATION AFTER CHRIST'S RESURRECTION

The ultra-dispensationalists, the followers of Dr. Bullinger of England and of lesser men in America, say that through the book of Acts until Acts 28:28 there was what they call "the Jewish church". Then they say that in Acts 28:28 Paul turned to the Gentiles and "the Gentile church" began, that "church truth" was revealed, and that at Acts 28:28 a new dispensation began. So, they say that, in this dispensation, baptism is out of order. That teaching is foolish, illogical and unscriptural. But lest some should be deceived by it we answer it briefly here.

I can show you that no new dispensation started in Acts 28:28. When you read the passage beginning with verse 17, you will see that when Paul got to Rome, he called the Jews together and out of the Scriptures he taught them concerning the Saviour. Verse 24 says, "And some believed the things which were spoken, and some believed not." Then Paul quoted the words of Isaiah 6:9, 10 to those that did not believe, and said in verse 28, "Be it known therefore unto you, that the salvation of God is sent unto the Gentiles, and that they will hear it."

Note that not a single hint is given of a new dispensation. Paul preached; some were saved and some were not. Those who were hardened in heart were specially warned. Then following his attempt to win Jews, Paul began to preach to the Gentiles. But that is an old story to anybody who has carefully read through the book of Acts, for that is exactly what Paul did everywhere he went! Look briefly, with me, at his record in Acts.

When Paul was first saved he preached in the synagogue at Damascus until "the Jews took counsel to kill him" (Acts 9:22-23).

In Antioch of Pisidia Paul and Barnabas went into the synagogue and Paul preached a great sermon (Acts 13:14-41). Then Gentiles wanted to hear the gospel, and some Jews and Gentiles were saved. But the mass of the Jews "were filled with envy, and spake against those things which were spoken by Paul, contradicting and blaspheming" (Acts 13:45). Then note what Paul and Barnabas did. Verses 46 and 47 say, "Then Paul and Barnabas waxed bold, and said, It was necessary that the word of God should first have been spoken to you: but seeing ye put it from you, and judge yourselves unworthy of everlasting life, lo, we turn to the Gentiles. For so hath the Lord commanded us, saying, I have set thee to be a light of the Gentiles, that thou shouldest be for salvation unto the ends of the earth."

Note that plain statement, "Lo, we turn to the Gentiles." Does that mean a new dispensation started in Acts 13:46? No, it does not. If it did mean that, then a new dispensation would start everywhere Paul preached! For always he preached first to the Jews, and later to the Gentiles when the Jews ceased to hear him.

In Acts 14 the same story is repeated; Paul and Barnabas first preached in the synagogue of the Jews, and then when "unbelieving Jews stirred up the Gentiles, and made their minds evil affected against the brethren," (vs. 2) Paul and Barnabas preached to Gentiles. In the nearby town of Lystra, Paul was worshipped by the Gen-

tiles, and later stoned! Paul and Silas went into the synagogue at Thessalonica (Acts 17:1-5) and Berea (Acts 17:10-14), and in each of these places he first preached to the Jews and was hated and driven out by the Jews, and then he preached to anybody he could. That was Paul's regular plan. He did there "as his manner was" (Acts 17:2) always. "To the Jew first" in every community, then to Gentiles.

In Acts 18:1-11 we learn how Paul preached at Corinth. He was first in the synagogue, but when chased out of the synagogue, he began preaching to Gentiles. Acts 18:6 says, "And when they opposed themselves, and blasphemed, he shook his raiment, and said unto them, Your blood be upon your own heads; I am clean: from henceforth I will go unto the Gentiles." Note that plain statement, "From henceforth I will go unto the Gentiles." But Paul meant the Gentiles in that particular area; he did not mean to begin a new dispensation, neither here nor elsewhere. The succeeding verses tell how he stayed there a year and six months, in the home of Justus, and how many were saved and baptized (Acts 18:8).

Now compare three statements of Paul:

At Antioch of Pisidia—"Lo, we turn to the Gentiles" (Acts 13:46).

At Corinth—"From henceforth I will go unto the Gentiles" (Acts 18:6).

At Rome—"Be it known therefore unto you, that the salvation of God is sent unto the Gentiles, and that they will hear it" (Acts 28:28).

These verses show that Paul, in every town into which he entered, followed the plan which he mentioned in Romans 1:16, "For I am not ashamed of the gospel of Christ: for it is the power of God unto salvation to every one that believeth; **to the Jew first, and also to the Greek.**"

And it was nothing new or unexpected that Paul should, everywhere he went, turn to the Gentiles, for the very day Paul was saved and called to be an apostle God promised to deliver him "from the Gentiles, **unto whom I now send thee**" (Acts 26:17). And later when he tried to go back to Jerusalem to preach, God said to him sharply, "Depart: for I will send thee far hence unto the Gentiles" (Acts 22:21).

There is not a shadow of evidence that God meant any new dispensation to begin in Acts 28:28. Paul did not change his preaching nor his practice. And even the Scripture from Isaiah 6:9-10, which Paul quoted to the stubborn Jews at Rome (Acts 28:25-27), was exactly the same Scripture that Jesus quoted to the Pharisees in His day, as given in Matthew 13:14, 15.

And yet on such a slender argument, without a single Scripture saying that a new dispensation was begun, some people, eager for a change, throw away baptism and some throw away even the Lord's Supper and even the Great Commission!

It is true that Paul preached to Gentiles, as he had been doing for some time before Acts 28:28; but he preached to them the same gospel, and he baptized them the same way Jesus commanded us to see that new converts were baptized, as we go "into all the world and preach the gospel to every creature" and continue "even unto the end of the world."

EPHESIANS 4:5 DOES NOT ELIMINATE BAPTISM

Short-sighted people who are not familiar with the context of Ephesians 4:5 which says, "one Lord, one faith, one baptism," foolishly say that it does away with baptism in water. Now it will simplify your understanding of that verse if you will read the whole short passage, Ephesians 4:1-7:

> **"I therefore, the prisoner of the Lord, beseech you that ye walk worthy of the vocation wherewith ye are called, With all lowliness and meekness, with longsuffering, forbearing one another in love; Endeavoring to keep the unity of the Spirit in the bond of peace. There is one body, and one Spirit, even as ye are called in one hope of your calling; One Lord, one faith, one baptism, One God and Father of all, who is above all, and through all, and in you all. But unto every one of us is given grace according to the measure of the gift of Christ."**

Notice that Paul is beseeching the Christians at Ephesus to be lowly, meek, longsuffering, forbearing one another in love, trying to "keep the unity of the Spirit in the bond of peace." He is trying to get Christians to get along one with the other. And then he tells them that all Christians have much in common.

1. They are parts of the same body.

2. They are indwelt by the same Holy Spirit.

3. They have the same blessed hope.

4. They have the same Lord and Saviour.

5. They have the same body of faith and doctrine.

6. They have the same baptism.

7. They have the same God and Father.

Therefore they ought to have unity.

You will notice that there is no discussion in the passage about how many bodies there are, how many Holy Spirits, how many different hopes, how many different Lords, how many different faiths, how many different baptisms, or how many different Gods. THAT IS NOT WHAT GOD IS TALKING ABOUT! Actually there has always been **only one of each** of the seven blessed things that all Christians should have alike. Some people would have you think that there were once two baptisms but that now baptism with water is done away with and that there remains only baptism in the Holy Spirit.

But if you will read very carefully, I am sure this matter will be clear in your mind.

There is only one literal, physical baptism mentioned for New Testament Christians, that is, baptism in water. Usually it is simply called "baptism." We say "water baptism," but the Bible never does, because "baptism" always means baptism in water unless the Scripture expressly describes some other kind of baptism. The truth is that for three or four years before Pentecost, John the Baptist was baptizing thousands and thousands of new converts in Judea, and Jesus and his disciples baptized other thousands, and everybody knew the term **baptism** and used it about the immersion of a new convert in water, after repentance. So baptism was simply the literal, physical act of immersing a new convert in water, picturing the coming death and burial of Christ.

Later the word **baptism** was used **figuratively** of several other things. For example Jesus, in Matthew 20:22, asked John and James, "Are ye able to drink of the cup that I shall drink of, and to be baptized with the baptism that I am baptized with?" Jesus referred to His sufferings, meaning that He would be immersed, covered, overwhelmed with sorrow and suffering. But note that that was **a figurative,** symbolical use of the word **baptized, and that it was not a literal, physical baptism. Literal baptism is in water, the burial or** immersion of a new convert, on profession of his faith.

Likewise in Acts 1:5 Jesus said, "For John truly baptized with water; but ye shall be baptized with the Holy Ghost not many days hence." John baptized with water, that is, literally immersed literal, physical people in water. But Jesus said, using that as a figure of speech, that at Pentecost the apostles should "be baptized with the Holy Ghost." In a figure of speech, He said that they would be immersed, covered, with the Holy Spirit. But actually the Holy Spirit is not physical, is not visible, and to say that one would be buried, immersed or baptized with Him is a figure of speech. Remember that that figure of speech was not often used about the Holy Spirit, and in Acts 2:4 when Pentecost came we are simply told that "they were all **filled** with the Holy Ghost." It is permissible to use the term "baptized with the Holy Ghost," if we remember that it was not a physical immersion, and that that is simply a figurative use of a term that was well understood referring to baptism in water.

So Paul was inspired to use the same figure of speech in I Corinthians 12:13 when he said, "For by one Spirit are we all baptized into one body." In a figurative sense, when one is converted, he becomes a part of the mystical, unseen body of Christians who will be called out at the rapture and assembled in Heaven. So as a figure of speech, one may say that he is buried into that body, immersed in it, becoming a part of that body. The picture is the same used in I Peter 2:5 where Christians are said to be living stones, built into a wall, and the wall is a spiritual house for God. In that fanciful and beautiful figure of speech the word **baptism** or **immersion** is used. But actually, of course, that is not in a physical baptism. It is only in a figurative sense that a Christian is built into a wall and covered or buried in the wall of a house. It is all right to say that we are baptized into the body of Christ, if you realize that that is only a figure of speech and not a literal, physical immersion of the believer into anything.

So you see that real, actual, physical, literal baptism means the immersion of a believer's body in literal water, symbolizing the burial and resurrection of Christ and the believer's portion in the salvation so purchased by Christ.

So when Ephesians 4:5 says there is "one Lord, one faith and one baptism," it refers to water baptism. And of this literal, physical baptism, there never has been but one kind taught in the Scriptures.

Of course that does not mean that no one will ever be overwhelmed with suffering, as Jesus said in Matthew 20:22, "baptized" with suf-

fering. But that is not a physical and literal baptism. Of course it does not mean that new converts no longer become a part of Christ's body, the church. But that is not a physical, literal baptism. Of course it does not mean that no Chritsian will ever any more be filled, covered, surrounded and overwhelmed with the power of the Holy Spirit as the disciples were at Pentecost. But that is only a figurative use of the word **baptism.**

God is simply saying that Christians have the same body, the same hope, the same Spirit, the same Lord, the same faith, the same baptism, the same God and Father and therefore they ought to be united. Ephesians 4:5 does not mean that water baptism is done away. It certainly does not indicate any change. There never was but one literal, physical baptism commanded for New Testament Christians and that one is still commanded.

HE WHO THROWS AWAY BAPTISM, THROWS AWAY THE BIBLE

If baptism is not for us, then we have no part in much of the New Testament. We would have to lay aside Matthew, Mark, Luke and John, since all of them give examples of people being baptized on the authority of Jesus. All of them tell about the baptism of Jesus Himself as our example. If baptism is not for us, then the Sermon on the Mount is not for us, for it is given in the same books. If baptism is not for us, then the plan of salvation as given throughout the book of John is not for us. Those who despise this blessed command of Jesus, that Christians should be baptized, and who say it is not for us, would have to do away with the Acts of the Apostles, since that is a book of revivals and baptisms. Romans, Colossians, First Peter, Ephesians, and First Corinthians must all be laid aside as not for this generation if baptism is not for us, for in all of these, the divinely inspired writers taught and referred to baptism as a duty of Christians.

Baptism is connected with every great doctrine in the Bible. If baptism is not for us, then of course the Great Commission is not for us. Jesus commanded soul winning in the same Great Commission where He commanded baptism. The one was given as positively as the other. If it is not right for us to baptize the converts after we win them, it is not right to win them. The Lord Jesus put both commands in the same sentence (Matt. 28:19, 20). So did the inspired Apostle Peter at Pentecost (Acts 2:38). Paul, the apostle to the Gen-

tiles, was inspired to connect baptism with the death of Christ and with His bodily resurrection. If one is not for us, then the other is not for us. The command to baptize, or be baptized, is not repealed or taken back anywhere in the Bible. So if I lay it aside, I must lay aside all the promises of God in the New Testament in the same books.

You can see that that is a foolish and wicked scheme of the Devil to get people to disregard the Word of God. Any man who throws away part of the Bible is a kind of modernist and is not to be trusted. If one man has a right to disregard the command of Jesus about baptism, other men have a right to disregard the teaching of Jesus on any other matter. As for me, I will have a whole Bible, inspired of God, all of it authoritative and reliable, or I will have no Bible at all.

CHAPTER IV.

BAPTISM DOES NOT SAVE—DOES NOT HELP SAVE

A favorite device of the Devil is to have men look to their works for their salvation instead of looking to Christ. He leads some to trust in their morality, some to depend upon lodge membership, some to depend upon confessions to priests; some he leads to trust in baptism. That is a fatal mistake. The unanimous voice of all the Scriptures is that people are saved by simple faith in Christ, without any act of righteousness, and baptism is never mentioned as a part of the plan of salvation. Baptism is an act of righteousness, for Jesus said in Matthew 3:15, "Thus it becometh us to fulfill all righteousness." Titus 3:5 says that such acts of righteousness do not save us:

> **"Not by works of righteousness which we have done, but according to his mercy he saved us, by the washing of regeneration, and renewing of the Holy Ghost."**

Baptism is certainly a good work, but Ephesians 2:8, 9 likewise says plainly that salvation is altogether a matter of God's mercy and not of our works:

> **"For by grace are ye saved through faith; and that not of yourselves: it is the gift of God: NOT OF WORKS, lest any man should boast."**

Salvation is a gift of God which is not deserved, is not bought, and cannot be paid for. No church nor preacher nor the individual saved has any right to claim credit when a soul is saved.

In fact, we are told again and again in the Bible that the man who trusts in Christ has everlasting life immediately. John 3:36 says:

> **"He that believeth on the Son HATH everlasting life: and he that believeth not the Son shall not see life; but the wrath of God abideth on him."**

"Hath" means has, present tense, in modern English. Likewise, John 5:24 says:

> **"Verily, verily, I say unto you, He that heareth my word, and believeth on him that sent me, HATH everlasting life, and shall not come into condemnation; but IS PASSED from death unto life."**

The same teaching is given in John 6:47:

> **"Verily, verily, I say unto you, He that believeth on me HATH everlasting life."**

In the Bible, we find it clear that people believed first and then were baptized. According to these statements from God's Word, they were already saved before they were baptized and any other man who trusts in Christ is saved that second, before he could possibly get to the baptismal waters. It does not take baptism to save one.

WHAT DOES "BAPTIZED FOR REMISSION OF SINS" MEAN?

In Acts 2:38, the term "for the remission of sins" is used as follows:

> **"Then Peter said unto them, Repent, and be baptized every one of you in the name of Jesus Christ for the remission of sins, and ye shall receive the gift of the Holy Ghost."**

Some people think that this passage contradicts the dozens of other plain statements in the Bible that a man is saved by faith and saved immediately when he believes. But when you use the word **for** in this passage just as it is used so many times in every-day conversation, you will see what Peter said. A man is arrested **for** stealing; one is grateful **for** a favor; one is blamed **for** carelessness; one is commended **for** bravery. The word **for** here does not mean **in order**

to or **to secure** remission of sins, and it is not rendered that way in any translation of the Bible we know of anywhere. The Greek word **eis** here translated **for** is sometimes translated in the Bible **against, among, at, unto, upon,** etc. It might properly be translated here "baptized **upon** the remission of your sins" or "baptized **referring to,** or **pointing toward** the remission of your sins," or "baptized **in** the remission of your sins." When one repents, he receives the remission of his sins. Then the obedient heart, following Christ in baptism, is promised the gift of the Holy Ghost, an entirely separate matter from salvation. What Peter said was that people ought to repent and then, after their sins are forgiven, they should be baptized as evidence of that. That is exactly what people ought to be baptized for, that is, to show the remission of their sins. That Scripture, then, does not mean that people ought to be baptized in order to be saved.

"HE THAT BELIEVETH AND IS BAPTIZED"

In Mark 16:16, believing and baptized are used together:

> **"He that believeth and is baptized shall be saved; but he that believeth not shall be damned."**

Christians are supposed to be baptized as soon as possible after they are saved. In Bible times they were usually baptized the same day, oftentimes the same hour of their conversion, even if it were midnight as in the case of the Philippian jailer in Acts 16:33. In fact, baptism is a public profession of faith. One can see baptism; one cannot see faith in the heart. It is natural to think of baptism following salvation, and Jesus said that those who believed and were baptized should be saved. He did not mean to contradict the rest of the Bible though, as you will see from the following words in the same verse, for He added, "But he that believeth not shall be damned." That makes it clear that the matter which settles it is believing just the same as is taught in John 3:18:

> **"He that believeth on him is not condemned: but he that believeth not is condemned already, because he hath not believed in the name of the only begotten Son of God.**

The above verse, John 3:18, settles it that the man who believes **in Christ is not condemned, whether or not he has been baptized. It also settles that the reason a man is condemned is** "because he hath **not believed." Salvation is settled** by belief in Christ, and only by **that.**

BELIEVING DOES NOT INCLUDE BAPTISM

There are so many Scriptures which plainly state again and again that the man who believes in Christ is saved, that those who teach baptism is essential to salvation cannot deny that. They try to get around these many Scriptures, however, by saying that faith includes baptism, that is, if one believes in Christ, he will be baptized, and that faith is not complete until one is baptized. However, in Mark 16:16 Jesus said, "He that believeth and is baptized," showing that believing and being baptized are two diflerent things. If believing includes baptism, then Jesus would not have added the word about baptism. If repenting includes baptism, Peter would not have said in Acts 2:38, "Repent and be baptized." No, they are not the same and are nowhere spoken of as the same in the Bible, nor is it ever stated in the Bible that believing includes baptism, nor that if one trusts Christ, he will be baptized. "He that believeth on the Son hath everlasting life" before he is baptized. Baptism does not save.

"BORN OF WATER" DOES NOT MEAN BAPTISM

"Born of water and of the Spirit" in John 3:5 is often quoted as if it referred to baptism. It most certainly does not, however. That passage says nothing about baptism, and in the same conversation with Nicodemus, Jesus repeatedly told just what it took to get this new birth. Read verses 14 to 18 and you will see that it is simply believing in Christ. "Born of water and of the Spirit" in John 3:5, is the same as "the washing of regeneration and the renewing of the Holy Ghost" in Titus 3:5. That verse plainly says that this is "**not by works of righteousness** which we have done, but according to His mercy He saved us," by this birth of water and the Spirit, or cleansing of regeneration and being made alive by the Holy Spirit.

Ephesians 5:26 tells us how Christ gave Himself for the church "that he might sanctify and cleanse it with the washing of water by the word." But this washing takes place inside. James 1:18 tells us that "of his own will begat he us with the word . . .," and I Peter 1:23 says that we are "born again . . . by the word of God." These Scriptures seem to mean that when one is saved, he is inwardly washed, cleansed, led to repentance and faith, by the Word of God, and made alive, spiritually, by the Holy Spirit. That, I believe, is the plain meaning of John 3:5, "born of water and the Spirit."

All of that happens on the inside of every sinner who is born of God. It is not on the outside, and is not baptism.

Notice the words again in John 3:5, "born of water and of the Spirit." The second "of" is in italics, which shows that it was not in the original Greek. Jesus said one must be "born of water and the Spirit," one birth. Jesus was only talking about one new birth, which happens on the inside. He did not say one needed to be born of the Spirit inside and of baptism outside, and did not mean so. John 3:5 does not refer to baptism.

"BAPTISM DOTH ALSO NOW SAVE US"

I Peter 3:21 is used as an argument that baptism saves people. Speaking of the ark "wherein few, that is, eight souls were saved by water," that passage continues:

> **"The like figure whereunto even baptism doth also now save us (not the putting away of the filth of the flesh, but the answer of a good conscience toward God,) by the resurrection of Jesus Christ."**

All difficulty about this passage disappears when you take the first plain statement in the verse that this is a "figure." The ark was a figure and picture of salvation, and the ark was certainly a type of Christ. Baptism is a "like figure" and Roman 6:5 states that it is a "likeness" of the death, and a "likeness" of the resurrection of Christ. Peter then continues that baptism does not put away the filth of the flesh, and says that it is "the answer of a good conscience toward God." Baptism, then, is only a picture, or figure, of salvation, and the man who is baptized should already have a "good conscience." In Hebrews 9:14 we are told how the conscience is to be purged by the blood of Christ. Then, after that conscience is purged "from dead works to serve the living God" and one has a "good conscience," he has a right to be baptized.

One who is baptized professes to have a good conscience toward God, with his sins forgiven. If that is not true, he has no right to be baptized and baptism is a lie and an empty pretense. Baptism is only for saved people, the answer of a conscience cleansed and forgiven.

"BAPTIZED INTO CHRIST"

Some people have been troubled by the phrase "baptized into Christ" in Galatians 3:27, which reads:

"For as many of you as have been baptized into Christ have put on Christ."

However, that is very clear if you read the verse before it and the rest of the context. Verse 26 says plainly, "For ye are all the children of God BY FAITH in Christ Jesus." The whole book of Galatians is written to prove that people are saved not by works, but by faith.

"Baptized into Christ" should read "baptized unto Christ" and is often so translated. The same Greek word, **eis**, translated in our King James Version **into** in this particular verse, is translated in verses 23 and 24 of the same chapter, **unto**. It is translated **unto** in scores of cases, **to** in many others, and **for** in many cases.

Compare "baptized into Christ" in Galatians 3:27 and "baptized into Jesus Christ" in Romans 6:3 with a phrase just like them in I Corinthians 10:2—"baptized unto Moses." The word **unto** is a translation of the same Greek word **eis** as **into** in the other passages. If the covering of Israel in the cloud and Red Sea did not put Israel into Moses, then baptism does not, of course, put one into Christ. Rather baptism points "unto" Christ, of course.

What the Lord says here is that as many as have been baptized for Christ, or pointing toward Christ, or picturing Christ, have publicly claimed Him before the world as their Saviour. I Peter 3:21 plainly states that baptism is a figure or picture. Romans 6:5 says twice that baptism is a "likeness" of the death and resurrection of Christ and also pictures the new life which the Christians plan to live. Colossians 2:12 tells us the same thing. A person then should be baptized unto Christ, that is, for Christ and to picture the change of heart which he already has by faith in Christ. This Scripture simply bears out the many, many plain statements of the Scripture that one is saved by faith, and puts on in figure and likeness, before the world, what already God has put in the heart. God puts the light in us, we should let it shine. God works in us our salvation, and we are commanded to work it out. (Phil. 2:12, 13).

"ARISE AND BE BAPTIZED AND WASH AWAY THY SINS"

Our friends who claim that baptism saves, or that one cannot be saved without baptism, sometimes quote Acts 22:16 as evidence that baptism saves:

"And now why tarriest thou? arise, and be baptized, and wash away thy sins, calling on the name of the Lord."

Compare this with the Lord's account of what happened, as given in Acts 9:17. Ananias said:

"Brother Saul, the Lord, even Jesus, that appeared unto thee in the way as thou camest, hath sent me, that thou mightest receive thy sight, and be filled with the Holy Ghost."

Remember that baptism is a figure, or picture, according to I Peter 3:21 and Romans 6:5. When Paul quoted, "Wash away thy sins," he certainly meant to use figurative language. Baptism is a figure as the Lord has told us. Compare this language with Matthew 26:26, 28 where Jesus said, "This is my body" . . . and "This is my blood." Jesus certainly meant, "This represents my body and my blood." "Be baptized, and wash away thy sins," certainly means, be baptized to picture the washing away of your sins. That is what baptism always does picture. Paul did not mean in Acts 22:16 to teach a different plan of salvation from that one he gave the jailer in Acts 16:31, "Believe on the Lord Jesus Christ, and thou shalt be saved." Nor did he mean Acts 22:16 to contradict Acts 13:39 where he told the people at Antioch, "And by him all that BELIEVE are justified from all things." (Already saved without baptism!)

The man who depends on baptism to save him will go down in the water a dry sinner and will come up a wet sinner, but he need expect no change of heart in that water. Baptism is to picture a change of heart which happens when one trusts in Christ.

OLD TESTAMENT SAINTS SAVED BY FAITH, WITHOUT BAPTISM

We have the record of many people in the Bible who were saved without baptism. I remind you that God has never had but one plan of salvation. In the Old Testament it was "not possible that the blood of bulls and of goats should take away sins" (Hebrews 10:4). In fact, the eleventh chapter of Hebrews tells us of case after case of people in the Old Testament times who were saved by faith. Acts 10:43 makes clear that the only plan of salvation taught in the Old Testament was by faith in Christ, just as it was preached in the New Testament. There, Peter said:

"To him give all the prophets witness, that through his name whosoever believeth in him shall receive remission of sins."

Remember, there never was any plan of salvation but by faith. Every Old Testament sacrifice and ceremony was a picture and shadow and type of the Lord Jesus Christ, "the Lamb of God which taketh away the sin of the world!"

Now, all of these Old Testament saints were saved without baptism, for there is not a word in the Old Testament about baptism and no record of a single person's ever being baptized before John the Baptist began it. Baptism, then, is not a part of God's plan of salvation.

PEOPLE SAVED WITHOUT BAPTISM IN NEW TESTAMENT

Since the same plan of salvation was preached in the Old Testament and in the New Testament, and people were saved in the Old Testament without baptism, you would expect them to be saved in the New Testament without baptism, and they were. In Luke 7:37-50 is the story of a woman, a notorious sinner. Verses 47 to 50 in that seventh chapter of Luke tell us plainly that her sins were forgiven her and that her faith had saved her. Read carefully these Scriptures:

Wherefore I say unto thee, Her sins, which are many, ARE FORGIVEN; for she loved much: but to whom little is forgiven, the same loveth little.

"And he said unto her, THY SINS ARE FORGIVEN."

"And he said to the woman, THY FAITH HATH SAVED THEE; go in peace."

Jesus plainly stated that the woman was already forgiven and was already saved by faith. She knelt at the feet of Jesus, trusted Him, and went away a saved woman. She was saved without baptism.

In Luke 18:35-43 we are told about the healing and conversion of a blind man. Verse 42 tells plainly, in the words of Jesus Himself, just how he was saved:

"And Jesus said unto him, Receive thy sight: THY FAITH HATH SAVED THEE."

Notice that salvation was received right there before he was baptized.

That is the same plan of salvation given throughout the book of John; in John 1:12, John 3:14-18, John 3:36, John 5:24, John 6:37, and many other places. It is the same plan taught by Peter after Pentecost (Acts 10:43). It was the same plan taught by Paul, the apostle to the Gentiles, (Acts 13:38, 39; Acts 16:30, 31; Ephesians 2:8, 9; Romans 3:28 and Romans 4:5-8). People were saved in the Old Testament by faith without baptism, were saved during the life of Jesus by faith without baptism, and were saved after Pentecost by faith without baptism.

That publican, about whom the Saviour has told us in Luke 18:13, 14 was saved without baptism. Standing there in the temple, he prayed, saying: "God be merciful to me a sinner." Jesus tells us about him then, that, "I tell you, this man went down to his house justified"! He was saved, then, without baptism.

THIEF ON THE CROSS SAVED WITHOUT BAPTISM

The most remarkable case of this kind is the thief converted on the cross as told in Luke 23: 39-43. When that poor man turned to the Lord Jesus and asked to be in His kingdom, the Lord Jesus replied, "Verily I say unto thee, to day shalt thou be with me in paradise"! He died that day on the cross as we are told in the Scriptures and so could not have been baptized. But that day, according to the express statement of the Saviour, he went with Jesus to paradise. And some happy day, all who trust in Christ will see him there.

No, baptism is not essential to salvation.

TRUST JESUS FOR SALVATION

God has just one plan of salvation. It is not a process. It is not a series of steps. People are saved by faith in Christ, that way and no other way. Everything else that God asks of a sinner in order to be saved: repentance, prayer, coming to Christ, etc., is summed up and settled when one depends upon Christ for the forgiveness of his sins. One could not turn his mind or heart toward God (repentance), without faith in Christ. You cannot come to Christ without believing on Him. "How then shall they call on him in whom they have not believed? and how shall they believe in him of whom they have not

heard?" (Rom. 10:14). Confession by the mouth simply proves faith in the heart which has already secured salvation. God has no other plan of salvation except that promised in John 3:16, 18, 36; John 5:24; John 6:47; Acts 16:30-31. "Believe on the Lord Jesus Christ and thou shalt be saved." Baptism follows, should follow immediately, but is not a part of God's plan of salvation. When you are baptized, be sure that fact is made clear to those who look on. If you have this salvation, this change of heart by faith in Jesus Christ, then I beg you, follow Jesus in baptism as soon as possible.

CHAPTER V

NO BABIES BAPTIZED IN THE BIBLE

Since salvation must come, according to the Bible, before there can be Bible baptism, it is obvious that there is no reason for baptizing babies, unaccountable infants. There is not one New Testament record of the baptism of an infant. Jesus did lay His hands on little children and bless them, but certainly He did not baptize them or the Scripture would somewhere have said so.

In the sixteenth chapter of Acts, there are two cases where households were baptized. The first was the household of Lydia of whom the Scripture says in Acts 16:14, 15:

> **"And a certain woman named Lydia, a seller of purple, of the city of Thyatira, which worshipped God, heard us: whose heart the Lord opened, that she attended unto the things which were spoken of Paul. And when she was baptized, and her household, she besought us, saying, If ye have judged me to be faithful to the Lord, come into my house, and abide there. And she constrained us."**

We do not know who was included in her household. Nothing was said about children, and it is not even intimated that she was married. Certainly there is no teaching of "infant baptism" here.

In the case of the jailer, in the same chapter, the Scripture makes it certain that there were no unaccountable babies. That passage in verses 29 to 34 says:

> **Then he called for a light, and sprang in, and came trembling, and fell down before Paul and Silas, And brought them**

out, and said, Sirs, what must I do to be saved? And they said, Believe on the Lord Jesus Christ, and thou shalt be saved, and thy house. And they spake unto him the word of the Lord, and to all that were in his house. And he took them the same hour of the night, and washed their stripes; and was baptized, he and all his, straightway. And when he had brought them into his house, he set meat before them, and rejoiced, believing in God with all his house."

Verse 33 does say "and was baptized, he and all his, straightway." But notice that verse 32 states that Paul and Silas preached the word "to all that were in his house" and verse 34 says that he "rejoiced, believing in God with all his house." Certainly everybody who was baptized in that household heard the word and believed in Christ.

BABIES CIRCUMCISED, WHY NOT BABIES BAPTIZED?

It is true that boy babies were circumcised in Israel when eight days old (Gen. 17:12). But baptism and circumcision are two entirely different matters. Circumcision was for boys and men only; while baptism is for both sexes alike. Circumcision was for every boy or man of Hebrew blood, while baptism is only for saved people. Circumcision and baptism mean entirely different things. Circumcision meant that this child was an Israelite, one of the chosen race by natural birth. Baptism means that the one baptized is born again and one of God's children by a birth from Heaven. One has no right to be baptized until he is born as God's child. The Bible does not say one word about dedicating little children to the Lord by any kind of Christian ceremony, and certainly does not mention baptism of babies anywhere in the Bible.

It is a sad and remarkable fact that many earnest Christian people have followed Roman Catholics in sprinkling unaccountable babies when there is not one verse in the Bible to even intimate that it was the will of God! In the Bible, people were baptized after they believed and were saved, as was the case with the jailer and his entire family.

THE HARM OF INFANT BAPTISM

Baptism of an unaccountable baby does untold harm. For one thing, it leaves the impression that the change of heart is not necessary. It leaves the impression that the religion of the Lord Jesus is

a matter of ritual, not of personal faith. It ignores the Bible teaching that baptism represents the burial and resurrection of Jesus and the believer's change of heart. Worst of all, the one who is thus given a ceremony which was only for Christians, often is led to believe, in after years, that since he is a member of a church, has been baptized, and is a respectable citizen, therefore he does not need the change of heart, does not need to be converted, saved by the blood of Jesus. Whatever fine argument you may make for the sprinkling of a little baby, it is answered by the plain, indisputable fact that Jesus did not command it and it is certainly unscriptural and wrong.

We begin to see, then, why the Lord Jesus puts such stress on baptism. It is the gospel, so simple that every new convert can preach it. It pictures the plan of salvation. Yea, it safeguards the plan of salvation. If I change the form of baptism, I change the meaning of baptism, I change the doctrine of salvation. If I take a little child, unaccountable, who has not trusted in Christ for salvation, and without his volition, I put water upon his head and "baptize" him, I have taught an entirely different plan of salvation. I have said to the unthinking world that people do not need a change of heart, but that with a simple rite of dedication they have a right into the fellowship of a New Testament church. When I change the form of baptism, I have lost all the picture about the death of Christ, His atonement, His resurrection, the change necessary in the believer's heart and the change commanded in his life. When people go wrong on baptism, they go wrong on the doctrine of salvation. If people have a right to change the form of baptism, they have a right to change the form of church government, change from the New Testament program of soul winning to the modern program of education. Good, old-time Methodist people who believe, as John Wesley did, in a change of heart, oftentimes wonder why that strong tendency of modern Methodism toward teaching salvation by works, by character, by education and by culture instead of salvation by the blood! One reason is, they do not have Bible baptism, a burial of the believer with Christ, to picture to the world the great teaching of the plan of salvation. Sprinkling babies teaches against the need for a change of heart.

STAY WITH BIBLE BAPTISM

Suppose we even retain the form of baptism, but still teach it as essential to salvation as do our Catholic friends and as do Churches

of Christ or Disciples, Lutherans and others. When one is baptized, then, he says to the world, "I am saving my soul by my good works." The preacher or priest is saying, perhaps unconsciously, to the world, "The church by rites and ceremonies is saving this man's soul." The candidate baptized, the preacher or priest, and the onlookers alike all miss the blessed, blessed teaching that Christ died for our sins, that men are saved simply by faith in His shed blood, that a deep-seated, fundamental change has been made in the heart of the believer, called the new birth. BIBLE BAPTISM IS GOD'S SAFEGUARD AROUND SOUND DOCTRINE ON THE PLAN OF SALVATION. That is the reason if baptism was not done the right way, or if it was done with the right method, but without the scriptural teaching in the minds of the people, it should be done again, as Paul baptized the second time those converts at Ephesus as told in Acts 19:1-6. Let us stay with the Bible as to the form and meaning of baptism and baptize only those who have a Bible right to baptism, that is, saved people. Certainly baptism of babies is unscriptural, dangerous and wrong.

CHAPTER VI.

THE FORM OF BAPTISM

The form of baptism is very clear from the Bible. Let us notice the plain teaching of the Scripture about this matter.

1. The form of baptism requires WATER. John the Baptist said, "I indeed baptize you with water" (Matt. 3:11; Mark 1:8; Luke 3:16; John 1:26, 33). A Bible baptism requires water. The word translated **with** in the above verse is usually translated **in.** The meaning here is, "I baptize you in water," though the King James version does not make that clear. But certainly, Bible baptism requires water.

2. New Testament baptism requires MUCH WATER. John 3:23 says, "John also was baptizing in Aenon near to Salim, **because there was much water there."**

3. New Testament baptism requires a GOING DOWN INTO THE WATER. Acts 8:38 says: "And he commanded the chariot to stand still: and **they went down both into the water, both Philip and the**

eunuch; and he baptized him." We see why much water is required, for it should be enough water for both the one baptized and the person who performs this beautiful ceremony to go together down into the water.

4. The Bible requires a BURIAL IN WATER. We are told in Romans 6:4

> **"Therefore we are buried with him by baptism into death: that like as Christ was raised up from the dead by the glory of the Father, even so we also should walk in newness of life."**

The following verse, Romans 6:5, says that baptism is a planting. Colossians 2:12 again specifically states that baptism is a burial.

> **"Buried with him in baptism, wherein also ye are risen with him through the faith of the operation of God, who hath raised him from the dead."**

5. New Testament baptism requires next a RESURRECTION FROM THE WATER. That was taught in the above Scriptures and especially in Romans 6:5.

> **"For if we have been planted together in the likeness of his death, we shall be also in the likeness of his resurrection."**

6. The last element in New Testament baptism is COMING UP STRAIGHTWAY OUT OF THE WATER to meet the smile of a heavenly Father who is pleased, and to walk in the joy of the Holy Spirit who fills the obedient Christian. So it was when Jesus was baptized, as we are told in Matthew 3:16, 17.

> **"And Jesus, when he was baptized, went up straightway out of the water: and, lo, the heavens were opened unto him, and he saw the Spirit of God descending like a dove, and lighting upon him: And lo a voice from heaven, saying, This is my beloved Son, in whom I am well pleased."**

Bible baptism, then, requires (1) WATER, (2) MUCH WATER, (3) GOING DOWN INTO THE WATER, (4) A BURIAL IN THE WATER, (5) RESURRECTION FROM THE WATER, (6) COMING UP OUT OF THE WATER! If you would be baptized as Jesus was,

baptized as He commanded us to be when He said about His own baptism, "Thus it becometh us to fulfil all righteousness," (Matthew 3:15), then plainly, dear child of God, here is the way!

SPRINKLING AND POURING ARE NOT BIBLE BAPTISM

Although the word **sprinkle** is used a number of times in the New Testament, it is never used about baptism. And the word which is translated **baptize** is never translated **sprinkle** in the entire New Testament. Sometimes people who use sprinkling instead of baptism, and can find no Scripture for it in the New Testament, turn to Ezekiel 36:25 as an evidence for sprinkling. That verse reads:

> **"Then will I sprinkle clean water upon you, and ye shall be clean: from all your filthiness, and from all your idols, will I cleanse you."**

They make a mistake, however, in not reading the rest of the same passage. Now read it again, beginning at verse 22, reading through verse 28. Notice from verse 22 that the message is to the house of Israel who are scattered out among the heathen. Notice that verse 24 promises to Israel "For I will take you from among the heathen, and gather you out of all countries, and will bring you into your own land." The Lord here is promising the restoration of Israel to their own land at the second coming of Christ. Then follows God's word that on these children of Israel He will sprinkle clean water and cleanse them from their idols. Verse 26 then tells of the conversion of Israel when God will give them new hearts. Verse 28 says:

> **"And ye shall dwell in the land that I gave to your fathers."**

This passage is clearly addressed to the people of Israel who will be regathered at the second coming of Christ, into the land of Canaan which God gave to their fathers. It is not promised to Gentiles, nor to anybody during this church age, and is not a prophecy of baptism. This does not refer, then, to baptism, as sprinkling nowhere else does.

But what did the Lord mean when He promises to sprinkle clean water on Israel? Just this: in the Old Testament ceremonial law, God commanded water of separation to be sprinkled on people for ceremonial cleansing. It was sprinkled on the Levites to separate them from the rest of Israel, in preparing them to work in the temple, as you see in Numbers 8:6, 7:

"Take the Levites from among the children of Israel, and cleanse them. And thus shalt thou do unto them, to cleanse them: Sprinkle water of purifying upon them, and let them shave all their flesh, and let them wash their clothes, and so make themselves clean."

This water of separation, or water of cleansing, was to be sprinkled on the third and seventh day on people who became ceremonially unclean by touching a dead body. (Numbers 19:11-22). That water was also to be sprinkled upon the tent, upon all the vessels, as well as upon people, as you see from Numbers 19:18.

"Clean water" in these passages means not simply clear water, but water which is ceremonially clean. Actually it was not clear water, but as you see from Numbers 19:17, it was water and the ashes of a burnt red heifer, mixed together. God will make Israel ceremonially clean when He leads them to their own land.

The Bible foretells that many ceremonial laws will be restored among Israel when Jesus returns and sits on the throne of David at Jerusalem. The feast of tabernacles is an example (Zech. 14:16). Ezekiel, chapters 40 to 46, tells about the temple, the priesthood, and the offerings in that kingdom age. The Bible does not mention baptism in that time.

Notice from that passage in Ezekiel 36:22-28 that in any case they will be regathered first, then sprinkled with clean water (or the water of separation which all Israel understood) and then be converted, be given a new heart! That is not the order with baptism, for in the Bible, baptism always comes after conversion, not before it. Neither this Scripture, nor any other in the Bible uses sprinkling in connection with baptism. Sometimes marginal references on baptism point to this Scripture in Ezekiel. Remember that all the marginal references in the Bible are put in there by men, and are not a part of the inspired Word of God. Where those references were written by men who practice sprinkling, naturally they try to point to some verse to teach sprinkling.

WHAT ABOUT THE BAPTISM AND THE POURING OUT OF THE HOLY SPIRIT?

The disciples were baptized with the Holy Spirit at Pentecost. Peter in Acts 2:16-18 said that was the fulfillment of the prophecy of

Joel where God said, "I will pour out of my Spirit upon all flesh." It is reasonable for one to ask, then, if the pouring out of God's Spirit could bring about a baptism of the Spirit, why could not pouring water bring about baptism with water? The answer is of course, that God poured out the Holy Spirit on the disciples at Pentecost until they were completely covered as well as filled with the Holy Spirit. The Holy Spirit completely surrounded them. (In Acts 5:15 people seem to have been healed by Peter's simply passing by them.) So people might be baptized by pouring if enough water were poured on them to make it a burial, which baptism is, as the Lord plainly says in Romans 6:4, 5 and Colossians 2:12. However, since in Bible baptism they went down into the water to be baptized, and were buried, it is clear that they did not pour water on people until they were covered up. The difference is, of course, that the Holy Spirit was in Heaven with the Father and was sent down upon the people to cover and fill them, while water is not. The Bible very clearly shows the form of baptism, and no spoonful of water nor a glassful of water on the head can picture a burial and resurrection, as the Bible says baptism does.

WAS JESUS SPRINKLED, STANDING IN THE JORDAN RIVER?

Jesus certainly went down into the water of the Jordan River when He was baptized. Mark 1:9-10 says:

> **"And it came to pass in those days, that Jesus came from Nazareth of Galilee, and was baptized of John in Jordan. And straightway coming up out of the water, he saw the heavens opened, and the Spirit like a dove descending upon him."**

Jesus was baptized IN JORDAN and came straightway up out of the water. Sometimes our Methodist and Presbyterian friends teach that Jesus stood in the water of the Jordan River and that John poured, or sprinkled, water on His head. However, the Bible says nothing of the kind. If preachers are really sincere in teaching that Jesus went down into the water of the Jordan River and was sprinkled, or that Philip and the eunuch went down into the water and Philip sprinkled the eunuch, then why do they not baptize that way? Why do not Presbyterian, Methodist, Episcopalian and Lutheran preachers lead people down into the water before they sprinkle them? They surely know that Jesus, when He was baptized, taught us to do it the same way, for He said: "THUS" (this way) "it becometh us to fulfill all righteousness." The only answer they can make is that

they do not think the form matters, just so it suits the person who is to be baptized.

Another thing which shows the insincerity of those who sprinkle is that they preach against immersion, say that it is not taught in the Bible, AND YET WILL BAPTIZE BY IMMERSION ANYONE WHO INSISTS UPON IT, if they cannot get them for church membership any other way! There is only one form of baptism, as the Lord says in Ephesians 4:5. Jesus was not baptized three ways that day in the River Jordan! He said for us to be baptized "thus," that is, as He was. Some will say, "Well, I think any form of baptism will do, just so it satisfies your own conscience." No, dear friend, a "good conscience" will be one that wants to follow the Word of God and do exactly what Jesus said. If we do not do it as He said, it will not have the meaning which He gave. We are to please the Lord Jesus, not ourselves, nor others.

Great Bible scholars of all faiths, Protestants and Catholics, agree that baptism in Bible times was by immersion, was a burial. However, many preachers who have been content to follow the traditions of men instead of the Bible, say, "Well, the form of baptism doesn't especially matter, anyway," and so deceive the people. This book is not written to defend any denomination. I am simply urging people to come back to God's way and follow the Bible instead of the traditions of men. The Scripture repeats twice that we are buried with Christ in baptism, so that we may know that the baptism of Jesus in the River Jordan was a burial.

THE WORD "BAPTIZE" MEANS IMMERSE

If baptism is immersion, then why doesn't the Bible plainly say immerse? It does! The word **baptize** means exactly that. The reason it was not translated **immerse** is that the word was not translated at all! as you will see in the next chapter. When the King James version of the Bible was translated, in 1611, to translate the word **baptize,** giving its literal meaning, **immerse,** would have caused great embarrassment and confusion to the Church of England. Remember that the Episcopalian church was then, and is now, supported and its ministry controlled, in England, by the government. So King James instructed the translators, in such cases, not to translate the word, but to simply spell it with English letters and let it go. So **baptizo,** the Greek word spelled with Greek letters, was simply spelled **baptize** in English letters. The word **baptize** was never heard of as an

English word before it was so translated. There had been very little circulation of the Scriptures among the common people before the King James translation, since scholars read the Scriptures in Latin, or in Hebrew, or in Greek. When the Revised Version and other modern translations were made, baptism had become such an issue that no interdenominational group of translators could agree on how to translate it, so the word was left as it is, **baptize.**

However, the people who, even today, speak the Greek language know the meaning of the word and have always baptized by immersion. Greek or Orthodox Catholics have never used anything but immersion. How could they when the word, in everyday use, means immersion?

SCRIPTURES UNANIMOUS ON IMMERSION FOR BAPTISM

Everywhere I go, I find many earnest Christians who are amazed to see how they have been misled on the matter of baptism. In a Louisiana town a young woman, a bank clerk, a devout Methodist girl, came to me and said: "Brother Rice, will you give me some of the Scriptures which teach sprinkling for baptism? It is strange, but all the Scriptures I happen to know about baptism seem to teach immersion. Methodists baptize either way, but I do not happen to remember the Scriptures which teach sprinkling."

I was somewhat embarrassed, and I feared she would not believe me if I told her there were no Scriptures teaching sprinkling for baptism. So I said instead, "Suppose we get my big concordance and look up every verse in the Bible which mentions **baptizing, baptism,** or **baptized.**" So we got the book before us and began. She was amazed that there was no mention of baptism in the Old Testament. We read through every verse referring to baptism, and when I looked up, her face was as white as death.

"Brother Rice," she said, "somebody has misled me. I trusted them, I thought they knew the Bible and had Scripture for everything they did. I have been deceived." Breaking into tears, she ran into her room and lay across her bed sobbing. I was a guest in the home and that night she did not come to supper. But that night she brought extra clothes to the service and at the close, with others, she followed her Lord in baptism. The cry of that poor, misled girl who followed tradition, who had faith in men, is with me today. People have a right to know the truth as to what God's Word teaches about baptism.

CHAPTER VII.

HOW THE WORLD GOT WRONG ON BAPTISM

There is a strange text of Scripture in Revelation 17:5

"And upon her forehead was a name written, MYSTERY, BABYLON THE GREAT, THE MOTHER OF HARLOTS AND ABOMINATIONS OF THE EARTH.

By reading the rest of the chapter, we find that evil woman is certainly used to represent Roman Catholicism. Rome with its world-wide spiritual adultery or false religion; Rome with its persecution of the martyrs; Rome with its riches and cathedrals, art treasures, gold, silver and pearls; Rome, a state church, riding on the beast of the Roman empire (which will be rebuilt again under the Anti-christ); Roman Catholicism, centered in the city of the seven hills, is the great harlot, mother of harlots and abominations. Ecclesiastical Rome is this modern Babylon. Read the verse again and you will see that God has plainly foretold for us that all the false doctrines, heresies, and religious abominations which come to Christianity in this age are a product of Roman Catholicism. Many individual Catholics are not to blame for this, and I mean no unkindness when I call attention to the plain and unmistakable meaning of this passage in God's Word. I do so to call attention to the fact that Roman Catholics officially changed from baptism to sprinkling. One fatal doctrine of our Catholic friends is that they claim the church, or council, or pope, has the authority to promulgate a doctrine, which, they believe, is as infallibly correct as if taught in the Word of God. In other words, the Bible is not the authority and guide of Roman Catholics. They do not claim that it is, and they deliberately and purposely depart from some teachings of the Bible. For instance, the Bible plainly says that a bishop or pastor should be the "husband of one wife" (I Tim. 3:2; Titus 1:6). Peter himself whom Catholics claim as their first pope, was married (Matt. 8:14). Roman Catholics knew this Bible teaching, yet they deliberately changed it, requiring priests and nuns not to marry. They insist that they had a right to change it, since they say the pope and the church have the authority of Christ on earth. When Jesus gave the Lord's supper (Matt. 26:26-28), He gave the disciples both the bread and the grapejuice, or wine. For many centuries Catholics did likewise, and THEN CHANGED IT!

Now the Catholic priests drink all the wine (and it is really intoxicating wine) and the common people are given only the bread of the Lord's supper. Catholics admit they changed it, and say they had a right to. On exactly the same basis, Catholics changed from baptism to sprinkling, as their own authorities frankly admit.

CATHOLIC ENCYCLOPEDIA ADMITS CATHOLICS CHANGED BAPTISM

I have before me the official Catholic Encyclopedia, sponsored by the Knights of Columbus with the imprimatur of Cardinal Farley and given to the public library by the local council of the Knights of Columbus. On page 259, Vol. II, under the heading "BAPTISM, II, Etymology" is this statement:

> "The word baptism is derived from the Greek word bapto or baptizo, to wash or to immerse."

On page 261, Vol. II, second column, (b), begins the following passage which we quote word for word.

> "The proximate matter of baptism is the ablution performed with water. The very word 'baptizo' as we have seen, means a washing. Three forms of ablution have prevailed among Christians, and the church holds them all to be valid because they fulfill the requisite signification of the baptismal laving. These forms are immersion, infusion and aspersion. **The most ancient form usually employed was unquestionably immersion.** This is not only evident from the writings of the Fathers and the early rituals of both the Latin and Oriental churches, but it can also be gathered from the Epistles of St. Paul, who speaks of baptism as a bath, (Eph. V, 26; Rom. VI, 4; Titus III, 5.) **In the Latin Church, immersion seems to have prevailed until the twelfth century.** After that time it is found in some places even as late as the sixteenth century. Infusion and aspersion, however, were growing common in the thirteenth century and gradually prevailed in the Western Church. The Oriental Churches have retained immersion, though not always in the sense of plunging the candidate's entire body below the water."

Notice that Catholic authorities admit that "IMMERSION SEEMS TO HAVE PREVAILED UNTIL THE TWELFTH CENTURY," IN THE LATIN OR ROMAN CATHOLIC CHURCH AND IN SOME PLACES AS LATE AS THE SIXTEENTH CENTURY. Notice the

words "THE ORIENTAL CHURCHES" meaning the Greek Catholics and some others. "HAVE RETAINED IMMERSION." Roman Catholics changed from baptizing by immersion to sprinkling. Greek Catholics keep the original form, immersion.

CATHOLICS ORIGINALLY HAD LARGE BAPTISTRIES FOR IMMERSION

Visitors to ancient churches or cathedrals in Europe built before the thirteenth century, would know that this is true. But we would rather prove it by this official encyclopedia prepared by Roman Catholic authorities under the supervision of a Roman Catholic cardinal. On Page 274, Vol. II of this Catholic Encyclopedia, under the heading "Archaeology" are the following passages;

> "In the apostolic age, as in Jewish times (John 3:23) baptism was administered without special fonts, at the seaside or in streams or pools of water. (Acts 8:38)" . . . "Indoor baptism, however, was not uncommon (Acts 9:18, 16:33) and, for the sake of both privacy and solemnity, came to be the rule: while reverence for the rite itself and for the water, which came in time to receive a special consecration, gave rise to the use of a special font or basin for the baptismal ceremony, and at a later period, for the preservation of the water. With the establishment of distinctly Christian places of worship, this font became one of their important adjuncts. In the East it took the form of a pool or cistern, similar to those of the baths, often larger, and deep enough to permit total immersion."

NOTICE THAT THE ROMAN CATHOLIC BAPTISTRIES WERE ORIGINALLY LARGE ENOUGH AND DEEP ENOUGH TO PERMIT A TOTAL IMMERSION! Catholics changed baptism from immersion to sprinkling.

CATHOLICS ADMIT GROWTH OF "INFANT BAPTISM" AMONG THEM

In the same Volume II, on page 275, first column, the official Catholic history of baptism, in this Catholic Encyclopedia, says:

> "The passing of the period of adult conversion to Christianity, and the **growing prevalence of infant baptism** with

the consequent frequency of administration determined a change in the structure of the fonts. Instead of a basin below the floor level, walls of masonry were built up to a height of three or four feet to facilitate the minister's holding a child over its opening: or a font hewn from solid stone rested on the chapel floor. Immersion of children had come to be the rule, and as the practice was adopted, too, in the case of adults, the fonts were sometimes large enough to admit of their being immersed. In the thirteenth century, however, simple infusion came by degrees, to be adopted, and was generally used, the font became smaller and more shallow, and was raised from the floor on piers or columns. The older type of font continued to find favor in Italy, but in the northern countries the winter chill of the waters hastened the general use of infusion, and as this rite required for each person baptized, but a small quantity of water, the font generally took the simple form and small dimensions it has today."

Notice the statement "in the thirteenth century, however, simple infusion (he means sprinkling) came by degrees to be adopted and was generally used." Notice the frank statement that because of cold weather, and the "growing prevalence" of the custom of "baptizing" infants, Catholics felt free to change the Lord's way of baptizing by immersion to sprinkling for their own convenience. This is the origin of sprinkling and pouring for baptism and of so-called "infant baptism." All modern denominations which use these customs got them from Roman Catholics, who began them, as the Scripture so clearly prophesied in Revelation 17:5

> "And upon her forehead was a name written, MYSTERY, BABYLON THE GREAT, THE MOTHER OF HARLOTS AND ABOMINATIONS OF THE EARTH."

LUTHER, BREAKING LOOSE FROM ROMAN CATHOLICISM, KEPT SPRINKLING

Early in the sixteenth century, a Catholic monk named Martin Luther became dissatisfied with the unscriptural teachings and practices of Roman Catholicism and tried to start a reform within the church. He discovered in the Bible that marvelous doctrine that people are saved by faith, not by church membership, nor baptism, nor by confessing to a priest and doing penance. Luther was excommunicated and his movement led to the creation of a new denomination, Lutherans. Luther was a great and good man, but he did not com-

plete his reform and carried over into the new denomination many of the customs and traditions to which he had become accustomed as a Catholic. The Lutherans clung to the idea of a state church, and to certain of the rituals such as confirmation, and continued to use sprinkling for baptism. Luther believed in baptism by immersion and understood that the Bible so taught. Dr. Philip Schaff in the History of the Christian Church, Vol. VII, on pages 218 and 219 quotes Luther as saying the following:

> "'Baptism,' he said, 'is that dipping into water, since it takes its name from the Greek, to baptize, signifying to dip, and baptism is a dipping. Baptism signifies two things—death and resurrection: that is, full and complete justification. When the minister dips the child into the water, this signifies death; when he draws him out again, this signifies life. Thus Paul explains the matter (Romans 6:4) . . . I COULD WISH THAT THE BAPTIZED SHOULD BE TOTALLY IMMERSED, ACCORDING TO THE MEANING OF THE WORD AND THE SIGNIFICATION OF THE MYSTERY; not that I think it necessary to do so, but that it would be well that so complete and perfect a thing as baptism should also be completely and perfectly expressed in the sign.'" (Type emphasis mine, J.R.R.)

However, instead of following the Bible in practice, Luther followed Roman Catholicism on baptism. Our Lutheran friends sprinkle today because they inherited that custom from Rome.

EPISCOPALIANS, COMING FROM CATHOLICISM, KEPT SPRINKLING INSTEAD OF GOING BACK TO BIBLE BAPTISM

About 1530-33, the fat king of England, Henry VIII, became dissatisfied with his wife, Queen Catherine. We can sympathize with him, for he had been forced, while a mere child, for reasons of state, to take as his bride Catherine of Aragon, the widow of his brother, much older. We can understand how it was never a love match. Besides that, she did not bear him an heir to the throne. And to cap it all, he fell in love with Anne Boleyn. He applied to the pope for a divorce from Catherine, his elderly, barren, and unloved wife. The pope refused, partly because of the strict Catholic teaching against divorce, and partly because that his strongest supporter in the world at that time was the Catholic monarch, Philip, King of Spain, and brother of Catherine, Henry's wife. The pope dared not lose the

friendship of the strongest king in Europe. There had been much unrest in England over corrupt practices among the Catholic clergy and dissatisfaction with Catholic rule. So Henry VIII promptly threatened to make the English branch of the Roman Catholic church independent. That was soon done and the "Anglican Church," or the English Episcopal denomination was born. The Episcopalians retained many of the forms of Catholicism. They followed the customs of sprinkling and "infant baptism" which had originated in the Roman Catholic church, and to which they were all accustomed.

THE NEW MEDIEVAL AND MODERN HISTORY by Samuel Bannister Harding, Page 345, gives the following account of the origin of the English, or Episcopalian Church:

> "The actual separation from Rome came from the desire of Henry VIII to have his marriage with Catherine of Aragon, with whom he had lived for 18 years, declared void, in order that he might marry Anne Boleyn, with whom he was infatuated; When the Pope refused to grant the annulment of his marriage, Henry obtained his divorce from a court of the English Church, presided over by Cranmer, his Archbishop of Canterbury. In 1533 he proclaimed Anne queen, in defiance of the Pope.
>
> "In November, 1534, the separation from Rome was made complete by the Act of Supremacy, passed by Parliament."

Episcopalians are sprinkled today because when they came out from Roman Catholicism they retained that form which the Catholics had adopted after doing away with the Bible form of baptism by immersion. They teach the sprinkling of babies and make it a part of the plan of salvation as their Catholic forefathers did.

EPISCOPAL PRAYER BOOK REQUIRED IMMERSION, EVEN OF BABIES UNLESS WEAK

Earnest men tried to break with Roman Catholic practice and doctrine when the English church became independent, but tradition was too strong. The first Episcopalian or English church Prayer Book, adopted 1549, provided for baptism by immersion even of babies. That rubric under the heading "Public Baptism of Infants," says:

> "Then the priest shall take the child in his hands, and ask the name; and naming the child SHALL DIP IT IN THE WATER THRICE. First dipping the right side; second, the left

side; the third time dipping the face toward the font; so it be discreetly and warily done, saying,

" 'I baptise thee in the name of the Father, and of the Son, and of the Holy Ghost, Amen.'

"And if the child be weak, it shall suffice to pour water upon it, saying the aforesaid words." (Type emphasis mine, J.R.R.)

In the prayerbook as revised in 1662 the above was changed to provide for dipping babies only once, "If they shall certify him that the child may well endure it." It was this English prayer book that John Wesley later followed, baptizing by immersion unless "certified that the child was weak." At this time the custom was already established to do it the easier and unscriptural way, and so they do it today, though the Prayer Book still stays concerning "the baptism of such as are of riper years," as well as of babies, that the priest or minister

"shall dip him in the water or pour water upon him, saying," etc.

Methodists will see how their "Discipline" was patterned after this, though they, like the Episcopalians, follow the Catholic practise, baptizing in the Bible way only when people insist upon it.

WHY BIBLE DOES NOT USE WORD IMMERSE

When King James of England encouraged a group of scholars to translate the Bible into the English language, naturally the instructions he gave were colored by the position and teachings of the state church of England, this Episcopal church, which came out from Roman Catholicism. The translators were ordered, in the case of any word where the literal translation would cause controversy or cast reflection on the state church, to simply Anglicize the Greek word, that is, to spell it with English letters and not translate the word at all. I mention two interesting examples. The Greek word **deacon,** literally meaning **servant,** was not translated, but simply spelled with English letters and made into an English word, because in their Episcopal form of church government, one order of the ministry had been named deacons. Likewise, the word, **baptizo,** which has the plain primary meaning of dip, plunge, immerse or bury was not translated at all. It was simply spelled out **baptize** and made into an English word. That is why our English Bible says "baptize" instead of saying "immerse."

THE BIRTH OF METHODISM

An Episcopalian clergyman on a trip to America, became acquainted with some earnest people of Moravian Brethren faith, and so learned about that blessed doctrine of the new birth and was happily converted. After his return to England, he with his brother and a group of other earnest young men, formed what was called "The Methodist Society." This Episcopalian preacher became a flaming evangelist and started a soul winning movement which went around the world and blessed millions of people. His name was John Wesley and the people who followed him soon formed a separate denomination called "Methodists" or "Wesleyans." In America, the Methodist Episcopal church was founded by them, later dividing into two branches, North and South. They turned away from much of the formalism of the Episcopalians and Catholics, but they retained the Episcopal form of denominational government, the doctrine that staying saved depended on one's works, and they kept sprinkling for baptism and "infant baptism" as Episcopalians and Catholics did before them. However, Wesley plainly taught that "the ancient form" of baptism was by immersion and he used that form often, even with babies!

JOHN WESLEY BAPTIZED BY IMMERSION; SAID IT WAS "THE ANCIENT MANNER OF BAPTIZING."

The great John Wesley first made an effort to go against the tide of tradition and custom and baptize by immersion. However, he made the mistake of following Episcopal rules, "baptizing" babies, instead of only believers, as the Bible teaches, and also using sprinkling instead of baptism if one was "certified" to be weak! But he plainly admitted that immersion was the Bible way of baptizing, and used immersion ordinarily, though he was greatly criticized for it by his Episcopalian brethren.

Once, in fact, Wesley was tried in court because he insisted on immersion. He tells about it, himself, in "John Wesley's Journal," something of a diary which he wrote. In the "Popular Edition, Condensed," of this Journal, published by Charles H. Kelly, London, 1903, I read and copied his account of that incident, which happened in Georgia in 1736. Here it is.

"Wed. May 5th—I was asked to baptize a child of Mr. Parker's, second bailiff of Savannah; but Mrs. Parker told me, 'Neither Mr. P. nor I will consent to its being dipped.' I an-

swered, 'If you certify that your child is weak it will suffice (the rubric says) to pour water upon it.' She replied, 'Nay the child is not weak, but I am resolved it shall not be dipped.' This argument I could not confute. So I went home; and the child was baptised by another person."

September first of the same year Wesley records in his Journal the "List of grievances presented by the grand jury," delivered to the court at Savannah, Georgia that day. Number 5 of these grievances for which Wesley was tried was, as Wesley copied it in his Journal,

"5. By refusing to baptize Mr. Parker's child, otherwise than by dipping, except the parents would certify it was weak, and not able to bear it."

The jury seems to have disagreed, and Wesley left the colony for England. Another entry in his journal, quoted by Robert Southey in LIFE OF WESLEY AND RISE AND PROGRESS OF METHODISM, footnote, page 58 edition of 1871), in Wesley's own words, is as follows:

"Mary Welch, aged eleven days, was baptized according to the custom of the first church and the rule of the church of England, by immersion. The child was ill then but recovered from that hour."

Robert Southey, in the book mentioned above, criticized Wesley severely on this question of baptizing by immersion. On page 498 Southey says;

"Both brothers (referring to John and Charles Wesley—J. R. R.) retained the fancy of baptizing by immersion, after they had outgrown many eccentricities; and Wesley sometimes followed the mode out of condescension to the whims of others where he had ceased to attach any importance to it, and must have perceived inconvenience of the practice. One of the charges which the virulent Toplady brought against him, was that of having immersed a certain Lydia Sheppard in a bathing tub in a cheesemonger's cellar, in Spittafields * * * *"

Wesley frankly believed that the Scripture taught immersion. In his "Explanatory Notes Upon The New Testament," he honestly declared himself, specially when commenting on Colossians 2:12 and Romans 6:4, and when he came to those Scriptures mentioned bap-

tism as a burial. In that commentary as published by Carlton and Porter, New York, page 376, the note on Romans 6:4, John Wesley, the founder of Methodism, says:

> "We are buried with him—Alluding to the ancient manner of baptizing by immersion."

WESLEY FOLLOWED EPISCOPALIANS AND CATHOLICS IN SPRINKLING AND "INFANT BAPTISM"

Wesley had been taught from childhood from the Episcopal or English church Prayer Book that babies were born again at baptism, as that Prayer Book still teaches, and he never got away from this tradition of men. In his sermon on The New Birth, part IV, point 2, as published by B. Waugh and T. Mason, 1835, Vol. I, page 405 of "The Works of the Reverend John Wesley," Wesley says:

> "It is certain our church supposes, that all who are baptized in their infancy are at the same time born again; and it is allowed that the whole office for the baptism of infants proceeds upon this supposition."

Wesley was there discussing John 3:5, and makes it clear that the reason he "baptized" babies was that it saved them! He followed this reasoning of Catholics and of the English church of which he was still a minister and member, and gradually gave way to their custom of sprinkling or pouring instead of Bible baptism. Now, however, Methodist ministers argue against that which Wesley so stoutly defended and practised, immersion for baptism. How sad that men should follow "Babylon the great, mother of harlots and abominations of the earth," Rome, instead of following the Word of God!

JOHN CALVIN, FOUNDER OF PRESBYTERIANISM, ADMITTED IMMERSION WAS ORIGINAL MODE OF BAPTISM

History tells a similar story concerning John Calvin and our Presbyterian friends. That great man had a part in the reformation, went back to the Bible teaching that salvation is altogether of God's grace, not of our works, and is obtained by simple faith in Christ. However, to avoid making more enemies, he retained the forms of sprinkling and "infant baptism" as they had been established by

Roman Catholics, instead of going back to the Bible way of baptizing only saved people, by burial in water.

Great scholar that he was, John Calvin could not entirely break away from his Catholic training and tradition. He knew that the word **baptize** in the Greek literally means **immerse**, and said so, admitted that New Testament practice and teaching was immersion. Yet he said it was "of no importance," and continued the Catholic customs of sprinkling and even sprinkled babies. In that famous work of his, "Institutes of the Christian Religion," in chapter XV on Baptism, at the close of paragraph XIX, Calvin says:

> "But whether the person who is baptized be wholly immersed, and whether thrice or once, or whether water be only poured or sprinkled upon him, is of no importance; churches ought to be left at liberty in this respect, to act according to the difference of countries. THE VERY WORD BAPTIZE, HOWEVER, SIGNIFIES TO IMMERSE; AND IT IS CERTAIN THAT IMMERSION WAS THE PRACTICE OF THE ANCIENT CHURCH."!!! (Type emphasis mine, J. R. R.)

Our Presbyterian friends, saying that what Jesus did and commanded about the form of baptism "is of no importance," have followed the Catholic example away from the Bible!

WHY GREEK CATHOLICS STILL BAPTIZE BY IMMERSION

You can very easily see that the Roman Catholic church has led most of the world away from the Bible form and doctrine of baptism. It is an interesting fact that Greek Catholics have always baptized by immersion, as they do today. Greek Catholics and Roman Catholics were the two sections in the "Great Schism" which split the Old Catholic Church, in the year 1054. Roman Catholics, you remember, did not make any essential change in the form of baptism until in the 13th century, and at the time of the split, the whole of the Old Catholic Church baptized by immersion. Greek Catholics, or Orthodox Catholics have simply continued the form which they had at the time of the split. It is possible that Greek Catholics would have changed to sprinkling also, since so many of their adherents were in cold countries like Russia; but that would have been very inconvenient as the New Testament is written in Greek and the word **baptizo** plainly means to immerse, as Greek Catholics have always

Sometimes, after compromising on the plain command of the Scripture, they try to defend their disobedience with Scripture. Such subtle modernists may claim that baptism was for Jews only, or that it was only intended for the Apostolic Age, or otherwise pervert the Scripture, either consciously or unconsciously, to condone their sin. But the way to please the Lord Jesus, and spread His gospel, is to do exactly what He said, "teaching ALL NATIONS, baptizing them in the name of the Father, the Son and the Holy Spirit; teaching them to observe all things whatsoever I have commanded you." Then, we have His promise, "Lo, I am with you alway, even unto the end of the world."

There is only one course left for you, dear Christian, if you seek to please Jesus Christ. You must follow the Saviour down into the watery grave in the likeness of His burial, and then, raised in the likeness of His resurrection, come up out of the water, proclaiming to the world your faith in a risen Saviour and your intention of living a new life for Him.

Can it be hard to decide when His Word is so plain and when He has done so much for you?

CHRISTIAN HAPPINESS DEPENDS ON OBEDIENCE

Salvation is settled when one trusts in Christ and the believer has everlasting life, (John 3:16; 3:36; 5:24; 6:47). But a Christian's joy and fellowship depends largely upon how he follows the Lord. This is especially true about baptism. Experience joins with Scripture to teach that baptism brings great joy and peace in the heart. We find many references to rejoicing in Bible cases of conversion, the joy coming AFTER BAPTISM, or in connection with it! In Acts 2:41, we are told:

> **"Then they that GLADLY received his word were baptized: and the same day there were added unto them about three thousand souls."**

In verse 46, following, we are told about the same people:

> **"And they, continuing daily with one accord in the temple, and breaking bread from house to house, did eat their meat with GLADNESS and singleness of heart."**

New Testament Christians had joy when they were baptized. In Acts 8:38, 39 is another case of a baptizing and rejoicing:

"And he commanded the chariot to stand still: and they went down both into the water, both Philip and the eunuch; and he baptized him. And when they were come up out of the water, the Spirit of the Lord caught away Philip, that the eunuch saw him no more: and he went on his way REJOICING."

The rejoicing followed the baptizing. Likewise, in the conversion of the jailer and his household in Acts 16:29-34, rejoicing followed baptism:

"Then he called for a light, and sprang in, and came trembling, and fell down before Paul and Silas, And brought them out, and said, Sirs, what must I do to be saved? And they said, Believe on the Lord Jesus Christ, and thou shalt be saved, and thy house. And they spake unto him the word of the Lord, and to all that were in his house. And he took them the same hour of the night, and washed their stripes; and was baptized, he and all his, straightway. And when he had brought them into his house, he set meat before them, and REJOICED, believing in God with all his house."

HOLY SPIRIT BRINGS JOY AT BAPTISM

There is very clear teaching in the Scripture that Christians, after they obey Christ in baptism, claim Him before the world, may expect to be filled with the Holy Spirit. When Jesus was baptized, the Holy Spirit came on Him in visible form, as an example to those who looked on, and the voice of the Father from Heaven said, "This is my beloved Son, in whom I am well pleased" (Matthew 3:17). In Acts 2:38, the gift of the Holy Spirit is promised to those who repent and then are baptized for, (referring to, or pointing toward) the remission of their sins. There the Apostle Peter said:

". . . Repent, and be baptized every one of you in the name of Jesus Christ for the remission of sins, and ye shall receive the gift of the Holy Ghost."

Notice in the following verse 39 that baptism, and the same promise of the Holy Spirit which goes with it, is for all of us, **"even as many as the Lord our God shall call."**

There are many other Scriptures which promise the Holy Spirit to those who obey the Lord, or keep His commandments. Jesus said to His disciples in John 14:15-17:

"If ye love me, keep my commandments. And I will pray the Father, and he shall give you another Comforter, that he may abide with you for ever; even the Spirit of truth; whom the world cannot receive, because it seeth him not, neither knoweth him: but ye know him; for he dwelleth with you, and shall be in you."

Peter, preaching on the resurrection of Christ in Acts 5:32, said:

"And we are his witnesses of these things; and so is also the Holy Ghost, whom God hath given to them that obey him."

When Jesus gave the Great Commission to His disciples in Matthew 28:19, 20, including baptism, He followed it with a promise that when we do these three things, making disciples, baptizing them and teaching them to obey His commands, "Lo, I am with you alway, even unto the end of the world." Part of the happiness, then, and presence of Jesus through the Holy Spirit is promised to them who baptize as well as to those who are baptized.

How many times have I heard shouts of rejoicing at a baptizing! Many, many times I have seen God's power manifested when new converts followed the Saviour's command about baptism. I remember in 1931 in the great revival on the court house square in Sherman, Texas, when some 2,000 people gathered around that brilliantly lighted scene and 28 converts, the first fruits of that revival (for we baptized many times), followed Jesus into the watery grave and followed Him in the likeness of His resurrection. A Mr. Welsh, fifty-eight years old, a hard sinner, a gambler, a profane, drinking man, turned with deep emotion and said to his wife, "If I had extra clothes, I would have this whole thing settled tonight!" "Well," she said, "we can have your clothes tomorrow night." And they did and I baptized him. On Christmas Eve, he died, after winning many other souls to Christ. The Holy Spirit came upon the people and blessed the testimony of the converts as the Lord had promised, so that a soul was saved.

In this same meeting, an old man about sixty arose from the water and shouted, "Hallelujah!" seized me about the neck, kissed me on the cheek, and then weeping for joy he went to the tent nearby which was used as a dressing room.

In Decatur, Texas, in a marvelous revival which God gave us, a woman came down into the baptistry of the tabernacle, whispering to herself. "Oh! Praise the Lord! Praise the Lord!"

"Sister, say it aloud, if you like," I said.

"Praise the Lord!" she cried, "I have been wanting to do this for nineteen years!" When she was baptized, I heard her down in the dressing room saying over and over softly, "Oh, Praise the Lord!"

God meant for Christians to be happy, and you will be, dear friend, if you obey the Lord so He can fill you with the Holy Spirit. When I was baptized, a twelve-or thirteen-year-old boy, in that railroad reservoir at Dundee, Texas, the Holy Spirit came upon me with sweet assurance and joy. He was not in form like a dove so others could see, but there was no doubt in my heart that He came. The Father spoke from Heaven to me, saying, in some manner as He did to Christ at His baptism, "This is my beloved son in whom I am well pleased." The people did not hear that voice, but I did, for it was a still small voice that spoke in my heart. Rejoicing goes with baptism when we do it God's way! If you want to be happy, dear Christian, then follow the Lord Jesus who said, "Thus it becometh us to fulfil all righteousness." (Matt. 3:15).

known. So Greek Catholics in this matter did not follow Roman Catholics into the modern way of sprinkling instead of the Bible way of baptizing. Today they still baptize by immersion, their priests marry, and both bread and wine are given in communion, unlike Roman Catholics who changed all these Bible teachings.

ALL DENOMINATIONS THAT SPRINKLE ADMIT THAT IMMERSION IS BAPTISM

Christians over the world are divided on many questions concerning baptism. Some say that baptism is essential to salvation; others say not. Some say that infants should be baptized as well as saved people, while some of us contend for baptism of believers only. Some people say that sprinkling is good enough, that since baptism does not save, it does not especially matter what form is used. Some modernists try to do away with baptism entirely. But people of every so-called Christian faith agree that **immersion is acceptable as baptism.** Catholics admit they changed to sprinkling, but will accept baptism by immersion as valid. The Episcopalians, Methodists, Presbyterians, and others who sprinkle yet receive immersion as valid baptism and admit that it is Bible baptism.

STUDY THE PROOF CAREFULLY: THEN AWAY FROM TRADITION, BACK TO THE BIBLE!

Sprinkling used for baptism, and so-called "infant baptism" IN EVERY CASE came from following the example and tradition of Catholics who first began them, as they themselves plainly admit. No group of people ever began sprinkling or "infant baptism" because of any Scripture on the subject, since not a single case of either, as baptism, nor a command for either is found in the entire Bible! I beg you to study the proof of every statement in this book. If you will come with an honest, humble heart, willing to follow the Bible alone, God will clearly reveal His will and teaching to you. The only safe guide is the Word of God! Put away your prejudice, leave the teachings of your childhood, cast out the traditions of men, and you will find the Scriptures absolutely unanimous in their teaching on baptism, and as clear as daylight!